T0137504

RISING ABOVE
Your Life Journey

RISING ABOVE

Your Life Journey

RECEIVING AND GIVING GOD'S COMFORTING GRACE

Bette Mabry

RISING ABOVE YOUR LIFE JOURNEY
RECEIVING AND GIVING GOD'S COMFORTING GRACE

iUniverse books may be ordered through booksellers or by contacting:

iUniverse
1663 Liberty Drive
Bloomington, IN 47403
www.iuniverse.com
1-800-Authors (1-800-288-4677)

ISBN: 978-1-5320-8603-8 (sc)
ISBN: 978-1-5320-9334-0 (e)

Library of Congress Control Number: 2020905633

Print information available on the last page.

iUniverse rev. date: 05/12/2020

CONTENTS

DEDICATION

It is with much love and devotion that I dedicate this, my first book, "Rising Above Your Life Journey" to my husband Jim Mabry to whom I have been married under the term of our engagement as written in chapter 6, "Lemons at the Beach." Our mutual reliance on God has allowed our love to grow to a new and different dimension. For that we give God the GLORY. May that in turn be reflected in this book and give you, the readers, courage in your own lives and journeys, to grow in your personal relationship with God and His Son Jesus Christ, as enabled by the power of the Holy Spirit.

My dear husband Jim, I am humbled to say I love you, dearly and am thankful for the gift of YOU! <u>My guiding light</u>.

If it hadn't been for your interest in my completing this book and its follow-up book "Ugly Bears", along with your encouragement, "Rising Above" would have never been completed. Whenever my health has declined, you bring up the subject of the writing my books, knowing that will bring me out of my "slump" and/or depression.

It has been your goal that I complete the writing of my two books, before my journey on earth is completed. How sweet you are about it. Unselfish! That is why I have dedicated this book to you.

Completing the books is your gift to me. I love you, my dear one, for your loving me so and the way you have been my caretaker. You have truly lived up to the words in the chapter "LEMONS AT THE BEACH."

Jim Mabry at wedding of nephew Brian Finzer and niece Molly in lovely Cator Woolford gardens at Fernbank in east Atlanta May 5, 2017.

Civil War Indian maiden Mary Jane Cloud

<u>Key Verses of Scripture</u>

Following are two passages of scripture upon which this book and the second book "Ugly Bears" are based and written. Comfort and compassion are used interchangeably throughout both books.

<u>MERCY AND COMFORT</u>

All praise to the God and Father of our Lord Jesus Christ. He is the source of every mercy and the God who comforts us. **He comforts us in all our troubles so that we can comfort others.** When others are troubled, we will be able to give them the same comfort God has given us. You can be sure that the more that we suffer for Christ, the more God will shower us with His comfort through Christ.

2 Corinthians 1:3-5 NLT

<u>WEAKNESS AND STRENGTH</u>

Since I know it is all for Christ's good, I am quite content with my weaknesses and with insults, hardships, persecutions, and calamities. **For when I am weak, then I am strong.**

2 Corinthians 12:10 NLT

Wedding of Aunt Blodwen Davies Barnes (d), sister of Grandma
Haley, born in Wales. As a child, I used to stay at her house
a lot. My mom lived with her before and after marrying my
daddy. Recently, I inherited her wedding ring, which I gave
to my daughter Janet Mabry Jacobs. The engraved wedding
date of 6/24/15 is the same as Janet's birthdate of 6/24.

Christmas at big house in Poland, Ohio in early 1950's with
Daddy, Mom, Lois, and Bette. Note icicles and Saint Nick
on tree. Saint Nick from Belgium via Aunt Ruth.

CHAPTER 1

My Guiding Light

One of my favorite themes in the Bible is that of the contrast of the concepts of light and darkness throughout the Scriptures. If one does much reading and /or studying of the Bible, they will encounter that issue over and over in many different ways and forms as God teaches His people lessons about Light and Dark. **In my Dedication of this book to my husband Jim, I refer to him as "My Guiding Light."** After I used that term, I thought about **God being referred to as the "Cloud", "Pillar of Fire" or "Light" leading His people**, the Israelites out of the land of Egypt to the Promised Land of Israel. In our ordinary, everyday life, there is a strong **contrast between light and dark in all kinds of events of life.** When Jim proposed to me, as I wrote in the chapter "Lemons at the Beach," he clearly stated that our marriage would be guided under the authority and premises of our God or Heavenly Father.

In our early years of marriage, Jim exhibited qualities of optimism as we faced various issues. As time passed, we encountered many events that others would qualify as adversities or challenges in our journey as husband and wife. **As the adversities increased in frequency, our need for compassion from God and others increased.** In time, various individuals mentioned the idea that I ought to write a book about some of our adventures and how we had survived the circumstances over time. I would always say that it wasn't the right time to write a book about our life, but I would know when it would be the correct time. **Little did I know that God would direct such an undertaking and it would be very clear what He would want me to do about it.**

In those early years, I wasn't used to listening to God speak to me and hearing His voice and being obedient to it. As we traveled our life journey, I started learning more about that part of being His child. Meanwhile, my husband Jim seemed to be maturing with respect to listening to God more than I did with respect to certain things.

Over the years we had grown our family with the addition of three children, Janet, Ricky, and Cynthia. We had built a new house in Fayetteville, accompanied with lots of adventure and an accident with a horse injuring Jim and almost killing him. He had experienced the problems of unemployment numerous times. We, as a family, had dealt with the resulting financial disarray far too much, including the times when we had two mortgages to take care of when we owned two houses during the years of housing slumps. Some of these issues are covered in the chapters of the book. My father died during these years, a devastating event.

As a child, my **Grandma Conklin had been my mentor in bringing me to the life of a Christian.** Jim had been raised under the influence of three of his aunts in a Christian atmosphere and they continued their influence with mentoring me, once Jim and I were married. **Aunt Clio and Aunt Ruth were always there to help us and our children along that segment of our journey. We were so blessed and didn't even know it!**

Our love and respect for each other blossomed and grew accordingly, in ways that we did not expect as a new type of love matured in our marriage. A deeper intimacy became part of our life through the circumstances we encountered along the journey, as we raised our family of three children. This in turn provided the opportunity for our love to grow deeper and in ways we never expected, because of the closeness needed through the circumstances. **My health issues, including several near-death experiences required Jim to give his all as caregiver and me to receive as care receiver, in ways that required major adjustments on my part.**

Hopefully, after reading the two books I have written, you will be able to relate to me (Bette), my family and our strong faith in the Lord. Additionally, may you have a greater understanding of the need for compassion, the necessity of comforting others and in return receiving comfort yourself.

The stories are personal and true, written about myself and members of my immediate and extended family. The stories have not been embellished in any way. It is important that you keep this in mind as you read the books. In addition to the adversities in our lives, I have also written about some of the **blessings we have received very unexpectedly**. Some of the adversities are common, while others have not been. Subject matter includes depression, suicide, abortion, death, accidents, rare diseases, a family reunion, hobbies, and career changes. Blessings include children, grandchildren, and our Christian faith and its related growth.

The books are spiritual in nature, because I would not be able to share how we coped with some of these events without including my Christian faith. Accordingly, appropriate quotes or stories from the Bible are included within the text of the stories. However, they are not presented in a deeply theological manner, but, are done so in a teaching presentation format.

The books are written to encourage the reader to understand the importance of receiving the gift of compassion or comfort from God and others. Then it is the responsibility of the recipient to reach out and give the gift of compassion or comfort to others. It need not be the same gift, but the principles are what we are called upon to learn and share with others. The **books are meant to be motivational, for the reader to learn and then apply the principles in their daily living.**

In writing the book, I have **purposely written some of the stories without expressing my personal feelings or emotions. I have done that so that you, the reader may experience your own emotions** about some of the stories. As you read the stories, you may relate to a similar experience or the story may cause you to think of another set of events and then you may get caught up in your own personal feelings. That way, you the reader, may feel what you want to feel, rather than what you think I want you to feel. Also, some of the stories contain controversial material, (abortion, suicide, civil rights) and I would like for you to feel free to delve into your own personal feelings. The book is written for younger and older readers, as well as men and women. Depth of Bible knowledge is not a deterrent to reading the book. They may also be used by a small group for discussion purposes, with its members exploring their feelings about certain subjects, learning more about compassion. May "Rise Above" and "Ugly Bears" help you become a more compassionate person, in the future, in our world that needs to be comforted on a daily basis.

After all of the stories are presented, an Appendix follows with several passages of appropriate sections of Scripture for study and discussion.

When my Mom died it became evident that I needed to write two books. Deciding how to divide our story into two separate books was not easy. As time went on, it became even more difficult to make those decisions as my health worsened. There were times we didn't think we would make it to celebrate our Golden Anniversary (50 years) on August 6, 2016. We were ecstatic, when we were able to celebrate with a lovely, low key reception with friends and family on August 6, 2016.

If it hadn't been for Jim's interest in my completing the books, and his encouragement, "Rising Above", the first book, and "Ugly

Bears", the second book, would have never been completed. I considered dedicating my first book to my neurologist Dr. Douglas Stuart, whose words and advice were the catalyst to proceed with the entire book project. I also thought about several of my friends who helped with proof-reading and encouragement along the way. I have been blessed with help along the way with this project of expressing God's love by those who have encountered challenges and events for needing God's comforting Grace.

Writing the books has been one blessing after another and a series of "togetherness" times for Jim and me. Since the conception of the books, Jim has been involved with supporting me with the project and been my primary cheerleader/encourager. He has been involved with supporting me both verbally and spiritually with the project. We have learned more about each other as I have written different sections of the books.

Additionally, I have become more aware of the stress and difficulties my illnesses have created for him. Thus, I have had to change in my attitudes and actions. This has changed our love for each other, growing it into something new and different, exciting in new ways. God is awesome in how He allows that to happen. I use the phrases "please" and "thank you" very freely with him. I am very thankful for his assistance in my care from him, that he provides so freely..... especially at 2:30 AM or 4:00AM.

Jim has been my caretaker in many different ways. He takes me to all of my doctor and related medical appointments and is involved with whatever medical care is necessary. His involvement has helped to make it possible for me to return home after certain hospitalizations, rather than being placed in a rehabilitation center. There was one incident whereby his input with the doctors helped to make the decision allowing me to return home. The doctors knew that Jim was well aware of my needs and what needed to be done for me.

Jim and some of my doctors joke about the fact that soon he will have earned his honorary medical degree. This would be in addition to his grocery shopping, cooking, housekeeping, financial matters, and hospitality degrees that he has earned since 2012. He has had to learn a lot of new skills over recent years, but I have had to teach him a lot from the bedside in a weakened state.

Let's go back to my beginning statements about Light and Darkness and our relationship with God. In doing research about the related Scripture verses, one of my favorite verses popped up:

Your word is a lamp to my feet
And a light to my path. Psalm 119:105 NASB

God's word provides light for whatever circumstances we are facing at the given time in our journey through life. It is our responsibility to seek out the Scriptures for His words that are written to guide us out of the Darkness.

In the book of Exodus, God explains to Moses in great detail how He is going to provide a way for His people to escape from the Egyptians. In that section of the Bible, the concepts of God being the Pillar of Cloud during the day and the Pillar of Fire at night, to lead the Israelites, are introduced. Exodus 13:20 NLT

The Egyptians could not see the Israelites because of the Pillars God had in place. God also explained that no one could see His face in Chapter 33 as follows:

"I will show kindness to anyone I choose, and I will show mercy to anyone I choose. But, you may not look directly at my face, for no one may see me and live." Exodus 33:19 NLT

Later in that chapter, it is written that Moses' face glowed with light. He had to cover it with a veil from time to time because of its brilliance. Once again, illumination was a factor in revealing God's will to the people.

Following are additional verses contrasting Light and Darkness in our lives:

"For you were once darkness. But now—you are light in the Lord. Live as children of the light." Ephesians 5:8 NIV

"You are all sons of the light and sons of the day. We do not belong to the night or to the darkness." 1 Thess. 5:5 NIV

I have referred to Jim as My Guiding Light giving consideration to these Scripture references from both the Old and New Testaments of the Bible. In the midst of the Darkness of my illnesses and the difficult times associated with them, Jim was my Guide and Protector as I traveled the difficult pathways of the journeys I was on at the time.

Quotes to Ponder

- **When we put our problems in God's Hands, He puts His presence in our Hearts.**
- **Inner peace begins the moment you choose not to allow another person or event to control your emotions.**
- **Your courage gives the rest of us hope.**

Lois and Bette dressed as pigs for Halloween, 1949

Lois and Bette singing on front porch 1951. Lois
is singing. Bette is just looking.

Lois and Bette with majorette dolls that Lois rode down the stairs

Easter 1955, Poland. Lois and Bette's outfits were the
same in every detail, before moving to Charlotte.

CHAPTER 2

"Comfort, Comfort, My People,"

Says your God" Isaiah 40:1 NLT

Over the years I have heard phrases directed to us, such as:

"What else can happen to you, or to your family?"

"I don't believe it!"

"You must feel like Job!"

"Sometimes life just isn't fair!"

"There must be a dark cloud following you around!"

And, many other clichés.

Sometimes, I have been able to laugh the comments off. Other times I have had to hide the tears and my feelings. And, depending on who is making the comment and whoever else is around, my response may have varied quite a bit. To be very honest, my answer may have also depended on where my heart was spiritually with the

Lord at the time. Likewise, if you are totally honest, if you have been confronted with such questions or comments, you would probably have answered in similar ways.

My husband Jim and I have faced many adversities, challenges, problems, or whatever else you may want to call them during our journey together as husband and wife. We have raised our three children and been involved with the lives of our grandchildren in many different roles. **In our wildest dreams, we never anticipated that we would travel many of the roads and pathways that have been part of our journey.** The one constant has been that our faith in Jesus Christ has grown as we have encountered each challenge and been given opportunities to grow spiritually as Christians. At this point in time **we have been married for fifty-three years, having joined our hearts as one in 1966.**

Some of these issues are common to most people as life-changing events and are part of our natural maturing process. However, we have encountered numerous events that are not so common or we have dealt with them many times over, with variations to the same problems. What has sustained us has been God's comforting Grace. As I have reflected over the past, I have realized that **God has comforted us with His Compassion**. Other individuals have been part of that process. As we have been **recipients of that Godly Grace, we have learned to comfort others with God's Grace according to the Scriptures.** The purpose of this book is to encourage you to reach out to others and comfort them in their hours of need in a Christ-like manner.

This book is written, using Scriptures to illustrate God's intentions of how we are to comfort others, as He has comforted us in our many different types of need. Included are personal true stories about our family. None of the stories are embellished. If personal names of individuals need to be changed, I have indicated so in the individual stories.

Writing the book has been a process much longer than I had anticipated. Our one daughter developed epilepsy with multiple seizures on a daily basis, which necessitated her moving in with us. Also, my mom died unexpectedly, and that required much time to take care of her estate. All of these events have had a bearing on which stories to include in the book.

Some of the topics that are included in the book, which illustrate God's comforting Grace in our lives are:

- Permanent injuries at the hands of a drunk driver
- Auto-immune diseases
- Prayers of Thanksgiving
- Facing an Abortion decision
- Loss of a loved one to Suicide
- Grandparents
- Family reunion times
- Working for God
- A horse accident
- Death of a friend in Iraq
- Old-maid aunts
- Spring Break at the beach
- Epilepsy
- Prison Ministry
- Reaching out to others in the workplace

As you may note, the topics include subjects other than illness and death. Often, we only think of reaching out to others at those times, but there are many other life events that we are called upon to extend God's comforting Grace. **May these stories help to expand your opportunities to reach out with a heart of Compassion**.

In the book of *Ecclesiastes 9:12 NLT,* King Solomon says that *"People can never predict when hard times might come. Like fish in a net or birds in a snare, people are often caught by sudden tragedy." NLT*

In the following verse, Solomon once again points out that nothing is certain in life: *"Enjoy prosperity while you can. But when hard times strike, realize that both come from God. That way you will realize that nothing is certain in this life." Eccl 7:14 NLT*

In an earlier passage, Solomon observes that "there is a time for everything, no matter what we face in life. Eccl 3:1-8, 11 NLT

1. There is a time for everything,
   A season for every activity under heaven.

2. A time to be born and a time to die.
   A time to plant and a time to harvest.

3. A time to kill and a time to heal.
   A time to tear down and a time to rebuild.

4. A time to cry and a time to laugh.
   A time to grieve and a time to dance.

5. A time to scatter stones and a time to gather stones.
   A time to embrace and a time to turn away.

6. A time to search and a time to lose.
   A time to keep and a time to throw away.

7. A time to tear and a time to mend.
   A time to be quiet and a time to speak up.

8. A time to love and a time to hate.
   A time for war and a time for peace.

9. God has made everything beautiful for its own time.

Later Solomon expounds on the benefits of two people supporting each other in time of need and then explains the greater strength of three people uniting together. Once again this supports the purpose of this book of reaching out to comfort others.

"Two people can accomplish more than twice as much as one; they get a better return for their labor. If one person falls, the other can reach out and help. But people who are alone when they fall are in real trouble. And on a cold night, two under the same blanket can gain warmth from each other. But how can one be warm alone? A person standing alone can be attacked and defeated, but two can stand back-to-back and conquer. Three are even better, for a triple-braided cord is not easily broken." Eccl 4:9-12 NLT

Solomon's timeless discourse on wisdom and folly addresses man's timeless need for support from God and from his fellow human beings. No matter what we are facing in life, we have need for compassion and comfort from God and others.

I wrote this chapter after a stay in the hospital. While there, I read the book of Ecclesiastes three times, studying it carefully. One of the doctors attending me had a medical student accompanying him during rounds. The student noticed my Bible and markings in it. We engaged in numerous conversations, including his participation in some Bible study groups and my book writing. All of that led to the writing of this chapter. The Lord certainly allowed me to witness to this new member of the medical profession. We always need to be listening and be aware of such opportunities. How many of those opportunities do you allow to pass you by?

Bette and Lois dressed alike in formal photo

CHAPTER 3

Bette's Family

"The steadfast love of the LORD never ceases; His
mercies never come to an end; they are new every
morning; great is your faithfulness."

Lamentations 3:22-23 ESV

I was the first- born child of Cloud and Lorraine Haley Conklin,
being born in Youngstown, Ohio in August 1944. I was given my
mother's name of Elizabeth Lorraine Conklin and was called Bette,
spelled with an "e" on the end. Throughout school and my adult
life, that abbreviated form of Elizabeth and spelling of Bette caused
me an endless amount of trouble. But, as Mom said, it was the way
Bette Davis's name was spelled.

Family History

My mom was called Lorraine, because her father had served in France during World War I and he liked the name Lorraine. My father's name was Cloud, just like a "cloud" in the sky. It was a family name, which he inherited from his father, which was inherited from a Native American Indian maiden. She had married a Union soldier during the Civil War. After the soldier's death during the Civil War and after the end of the War, she volunteered as a missionary in the saw palmetto area of South Carolina, teaching the children of color, as they are referred to in hand-written notes, on the back side of the historic photographs.

My father's paternal family, the Conklin family, traces their beginnings in America all the way back to the 1640's, having come from England. Their history is interesting and filled with all kinds of tales, some of which are in American history books.

My mother's maternal family, the Davies (Davis) came to the United States in the late 1800's from Wales. Two of my mother's aunts were born in Wales. The Welsh heritage was carried down into my mom's generation and even into my generation. In particular, the cooking and singing traditions have survived.

My sister Lois

My sister Lois Elaine joined our family in December 1946. (She is two years younger than me.) My mother was determined to raise us equally and **give us the same opportunities in life with respect to just about everything**. That meant as far back as I can remember, we were dressed alike. On rare occasion, our outfits or stuffed animals might have been a different color, but otherwise, they were the same. Because she dressed us alike, we always had people asking us if we were twins. We were pretty much the same size for a long time, so it was not an unusual question to be asked.

- Two things happened to start to break down this "look alike" phenomena.
  - Lois was a rougher, more tumble person than I was. Accordingly, her toys became worn out quicker and more so than mine. As she has said, "her three foot high majorette doll's face was smashed in, from her riding it down the stairs!" Her stuffed animals lost their bows way before mine did.

  - When we were in high school each of us started sewing our own clothes, using the money we earned from babysitting to pay for the material and supplies. At the fabric store we each exercised some of our first attempts at independence by choosing different patterns and materials.

It is important that I share this with you, because of events that happened as we grew up and became adults, as discussed elsewhere in the book.

Both of our parents' desire that Lois and I be close with each other was accomplished in their methods of raising us. Granted we share many of the same interests, but we also serve others in many different capacities and manners. Additionally, **each of us suffer from auto-immune diseases and are there for each other in ways that we might not be otherwise.**

Moving Around

My earliest memories of a home was the two-story house built in the 1850's, where we lived in Poland, Ohio, with my Grandma and Gramps Conklin (Daddy's parents). They lived on one side and we lived on the other side of the historic structure. There was an open stairwell that divided the two sides, allowing our two families to be fairly accessible to each other. The house is now designated as a National Historical Registered Home.

While I was in the third grade, we moved into a home of our own, located about two miles away from my grandparents. **I missed the daily chatter and interaction, especially with Grandma.** At the end of fifth grade we moved to Charlotte, NC in hopes that the change in climate would help to improve Daddy's health problems with allergies. At the end of sixth grade we moved to Ft. Lauderdale, FL, since the climate in NC did not improve Daddy's health. Three years later we moved to the Melbourne/Satellite Beach, FL area for my parents' final move of their lives.

All of these moves were challenging and brought major adjustments to our lives. I realize that these were not easy times for my parents and that **they were greatly in need of God's comforting Grace for many reasons, with each of these moves**. I wonder how much or how little was available to them at each juncture of the journeys. As I have sifted through various paperwork, in settling my mom's estate, I tend to believe that times were very difficult and that **there was much loneliness**. For me, making new friends was awful, because I was so shy and insecure. The one constant was that I had my sister Lois to play with and have as a friend.

Employment

My father worked as an electrical engineer, in various capacities. He worked for local firms, national firms, and on a consulting basis. His last employment was with Pan Am, a subcontractor with the NASA Space Program at Cape Kennedy or Cape Canaveral, Florida. He excelled with this work and enjoyed the challenge and excitement of the United States Space Program.

During his last years he also earned a Master's degree in Business Administration at Rollins College in Florida, enhancing his abilities to manage the section that he was responsible for in the Space

Program. See the Graduation letter from his mother that is presented later in this chapter.

Recently I inherited certain papers from my mom's estate related to his employment history. Within those files, were the telegrams sent to him by Pan Am, offering him employment with his salary listed, along with the amount of the moving expenses to be covered. He was instructed to reply his response of acceptance via telegram. Also included was a letter congratulating him on achieving a monumental amount of work, in a short amount of time, for NASA under his management, along with notification of a substantial bonus. What a change from today's method of offering employment, etc.—the use of telegrams. His mother was very interested in the Space Program and excited that her youngest son Cloud was to be working in such a capacity.

Amongst the papers was a letter she wrote to my daddy the day the spacecraft Apollo 9 landed in the Atlantic Ocean. She wrote expressing her feelings about the event and her thoughts about the role each person plays in the success and/or failure of the progress of mankind in Space or other scientific endeavors. Following are portions of her letter dated Thursday March 13, 1969: (It was very exciting for me to find this letter from Grandma C.)

> *My Dear Ones— (this was her favorite way of addressing our family in a letter)*
>
> *I am thinking of you much this morning, my son, as I watched Apollo 9 splash down in the Atlantic. It was 9 a.m. out here and I was just eating my breakfast. It is 11 now and I just finished dressing. One of my neighbors came in just as I was watching them get on the ship. What a thrill it is each time! And, I like all others wonder the why and wherefore, but that has been true of everything that man has ever attempted. I had many thoughts of how much brain power went into the action and of how important each little nut and bolt and screw is and how important it was to have*

3 men congenial enough, brilliant enough to endure this confinement and all, for so long! When they took off and others also I think of "Nearer, My God to Thee." "Sun, Moon, and Stars, forgot upward I fly." Well, you see how it affected me—right or wrong! Of course I thought of my son and he is probably one of the littlest screws. He did his job. You see it could make a wonderful sermon. In the remainder of the letter she mentions that Gramps (Daddy) says she is in "high speed again" after being ill. Then she mentions that son George has been ill and her concern about him. Daughter Ruth has resigned from her position in the Congo, but they will be staying until son Richard completes his school term in May. Grandma is concerned about keeping certain news from grandson Jim who is the oldest grandchild and other relatives. Always the protector, Grandma watches over all. She closes the letter with her personal concerns about her own personal passing and death, giving my daddy specific final instructions beyond those that she had given him in previous years after Gramps had passed. For someone with as strong a faith as she had and believed we were on God's journey, the letter was very interesting and eye-opening. Now I know more about one of my personal heroines. (Grandma was living in California at this time, having moved there from Florida after Gramps passed away.)

I found another letter from Grandma to my father when he graduated from Rollins College, earning his Master's degree. Its contents are as follows: *Dear Son, When this reaches you will have reached another milestone in the Journey of life and I want to congratulate you and wish for you many returns of the day. Each year is full of experiences and if we learn our lessons as we must, we are better fitted to go on. Success does not come in a minute and real success is attained by doing day by day. You have certainly met your problems manfully even when you were only a boy and with the inspiration you have from your dear helpmate and three such children as the Lord has given you. (I assume she means Lois, Libby, and me.) The future must be bright for you. Keep the faith and feel sure you will always — in love.*

In another letter sent to me, on Dec 6, Grandma apologizes for not sending a Christmas gift. Instead, she sent a knick knack that I still have displayed and cherish, because it is purple, my favorite color and it is from her. She writes that she is "sending all her love that she has and the kind of Christmas that God in His goodness gave when His Son was born that first Christmas morning. I hope my dears that you reciprocate in kind and my love will continue."

Grandma Conklin

How precious are these letters that I found recently.

My mother

She worked off and on over the years in secretarial and bookkeeping positions, as well as in support roles when Daddy had his own businesses. However, when we moved to the Space Program area, she also became employed in that area and enjoyed the opportunities to learn totally new skills and applications.

After Daddy's death, she became a Pan American World Services, Inc. employee and became involved with international transactions regarding the employees. **Top secret events were daily "events"** for her. It wasn't until about a year before she died, that she ever talked to me about her employment. I was dumbfounded and overwhelmed. I can't remember much of what she told me, because I was so shocked! The only thing I know is that she always was interested whenever a missile shot went off. She would scurry out into our front yard and watch the shot, with her binoculars in hand, as we heard the rumbling sounds from the blast-offs of the missiles.

Spiritual Life

I grew up in a Christian home, but my Grandma Conklin was my mentor. If it had not been for Grandma C, I do not think that I would have had the basic foundation for my faith to grow from. Her **example and love provided the proverbial seeds for me**. My sister Lois will tell you the same thing.

During my Daddy's last few years, his faith grew and was a very important part of his life. I observed major changes in my Mom's faith after Daddy died in 1974. Faced with living alone for the next forty years, she depended on the Lord to take care of her. She also trusted the Lord as she dealt with Lois's and my health issues. She became **our "cheerleader" in times of adversity**! And, she reached out to others, serving as God's hands and feet in many different roles.

Education

My parents strongly believed that a college education was something they were to provide for Lois and me. Knowing what I know now, it was a **tremendous sacrifice for them**. I always remember thanking them for my college education over and over again, after I graduated. But, I never knew the significance of my words until recently. Today, I am thankful that I thanked them as profusely as I did.

My final choice of a college to attend was Western Reserve University in Cleveland, Ohio. The undergraduate women's college was Mather College, with a class of about 200 students. The entire research-oriented institution was a much larger university. Adjacent to our campus was Case Institute of Technology, which was separated from us by a single chain link fence. Today those two universities are combined as one – Case Western Reserve University (CWRU). **This setting provided an opportunity for me to become more independent and explore new avenues in my life.** I earned a Bachelor of Economics degree with a minor in Accounting in 1966.

While at Western Reserve, I **moved outside of my sheltered life** as a Southern, white Christian. **I was in the minority**, as the majority of the students were of the Jewish faith! There were atheists! And members of the Eastern faiths! There were also students of different races and ethnic backgrounds. I learned of cultural differences from New England and New York in comparison to the South. To many, financial matters were of no concern and to others, like me, we had to work jobs on campus to help pay for our room and board. I also **had to confront the fact that I was very naïve and very shy**. Additionally, I did not know that I was a person who **lived in fear of trying "new" things.**

After I married Jim, he went to college to earn his Bachelor's degree. I decided that if I was going to earn my Master's degree, now would be the time to do it. So, I went to Georgia State University in Atlanta, at night, taking one course at a time. I graduated in May 1970, with a Master of Professional Accountancy degree. This education prepared me to be able to pass the exams for certification as a Certified Public Accountant and practice as one.

Bette's Career

When I graduated in 1966, I began working with a national certified public accounting firm Pannell Kerr Forster, as a staff accountant. At that time, the "Big 8" national CPA firms did not hire females.

When I became pregnant with our first child Janet in 1969, I purposely did not tell my employer that I was pregnant until after raises were announced in 1970, because I knew that information would affect my salary negatively. This was in the **days before equal rights existed for women in the work place.**

I took the last part of the CPA exam in May 1970 in the "Pig Exhibition Hall" of the Georgia State Fairgrounds in Atlanta, GA. Janet was born on June 24th. Taking the exam, I was 4'10" tall, pregnant way out front, and miserable with no air conditioning in the

Pig Exhibition Hall. I hold one of the lowest numbered certificates in the state of Georgia – # 2171, held by a female.

After Janet and our son Ricky were born, I established an accounting and consulting firm that I operated until 1988. Then I became an employee of a stock brokerage and investment banking firm for a few years, learning a whole new area of finance.

Afterwards, I became a partner in a small investment banking firm, which was a culmination of all the experiences I had over the past twenty-five years. Unfortunately, all that **came to an abrupt end one day,** when my car was hit by a drunk driver and my body suffered permanent injuries.

As Grandma C used to say, "We are on a journey." Day to day, we never know where that journey will take us. If we place our life in God's hands and trust Him, we know that **He will take us where He wants us to be in order to fulfill His purpose for our life.** That is not to say that the journey will be easy!

Jim and I enjoyed hiking in wooded areas. Quite often we came upon forks in the trails and wondered, "Which path shall we take?" There have even been times when I have taken photographs of the forks in the road, because they were so interesting or intriguing. I am sure that you have also come to such crossroads in your life.

Sometimes we have **needed comfort and compassion on these various paths and it hasn't been there**. In turn, that has made the journey more difficult and lonely. Other times, there has been an abundance of compassion.

The Performing Lorraine

My mother's life included much time for appreciation of the fine arts, including the musical sector. As a young child, she participated in dancing and acting and was featured in locally sponsored plays, individually, and as part of acting groups. One photo features her playing the role of a darling kitten, along with other coy kittens. **Her**

father loved it that his daughter, Lorraine was talented enough to perform, entertaining others in the Youngstown, Ohio area.

Next, came getting a baby grand piano on the day before the Stock Market crashed at the beginning of the Great Depression in 1929. The piano retailer allowed the Haley family to keep the piano since there was no safe place for the retailer to keep the lovely baby grand. Mom began her piano lessons and pursued learning how to play classical music on it. The **piano was one of the last items we disposed of from her estate. It was acquired by a Hispanic family with many children and I can just imagine the joy the piano has brought to that family. The father had been the yard man for Mom for many years.**

After Daddy died, Mom really pursued her interests in the performing arts in an unexpected way. **The King Center for the Performing Arts was established in the Melbourne, Florida area for the purpose of bringing in well-known entertainers for the pleasure of the local residents and employees in the Space industry. Volunteers were utilized for supplying the necessary staff needs. My mom was one of those people who gave their hearts to this effort. She served on the ushering and front office staff for twenty-five years.** Often, she was active as the **head usher** for the day or evening's performances.

Excitement filled her voice when she told us stories about the different entertainers that she met and worked with. As I went through her files after her death, I found signed photos and promo materials from **Peter, Paul, and Mary, Yanni, Crystal Gayle, various performing military bands, the "Big Bopper", Little Richard, Henry Mancini, and many others**. Her favorite story was about **dancing with Don Rickels in the side wings while waiting for his performance** time. At only, four foot, ten inches, it was a real show watching big Don dance little Lorraine around. Mom enjoyed this time of her life for the twenty-five years from 1988 forward. It was fun, reading the thank you notes written to her from the various patrons, thanking her for her hospitality and care.

Mom also participated with a group of elderly women who did **marching performances**, with themes co-ordinated with the season of the year. In her early nineties, she was **just as spunky as could be**, out there performing with the others in her uniforms, up until a few months before she died at the age of ninety-three.

Have I been available to others when they needed grace and comfort? Have you? What did you do to help others?

Reflecting back to **Solomon's expose on life, there is a time for everything. This is a quick snapshot of my life and next will be a snapshot of Jim's life. Hopefully you will have an idea of our backgrounds before we get into the nitty-gritty of the book**.

Daddy at work shortly after graduating from Youngstown College
in early 1950's. He liked to wear bow ties and our grandson
Andrew Kenney has taken over his Boppa's collection of bow ties.

Daddy checking out electrical equipment

Daddy's graduation from Rollins College. His parents
Grandma and Gramps Conklin attended the event in
June, 1966, when he received his Master's degree.

My mom, as a child, in a drama group, dressed
as a kitty cat, squatting on a stool, in the second
row, to the far right, as a drama queen.

My mom playing her baby grand piano until near the
end of her life in her home, near the age of 93.

CHAPTER 4

Jim's Family

Jim (James Jackson Mabry, Jr.) was also a first-born child, being born in June 1942, in Summerville, SC to James Jackson Mabry, Sr. and Thelma Dee Haynes Mabry. At the time, Jim's father worked in the Navy shipyards near Charleston, SC where he worked in a **support role for the Navy during World War II.** Thelma felt lonely, being away from her four sisters and James' sisters back in Atlanta.

A Sick Baby

At the age of six months, **Jim became ill and was having problems with one of his arms. His mother took him to the doctors and they told her there was nothing to do but amputate his arm**. She grabbed him up, said no one would do that to her baby, and that she would take him to the doctors in Atlanta. The doctor said if you do that, **"your baby will be a "dead baby" before you get him to Atlanta**. You can't take a chance on going there!"

She took Jim home and told James of the problem at hand. They packed up their few belongings and headed back home to Atlanta. It was over a 300 mile trip, without any interstate highways, in a red 1940 Ford. At Crawford Long Hospital, now downtown Emory Hospital, in Atlanta, Dr. Daniel told Thelma to give Jim as much orange juice as she could get into him, to help cure the scurvy that was attacking his body. What Jim needed was Vitamin C, not an amputation! As Jim recovered, they moved in with one of James' sisters, Nell.

A Growing Family and a Dairy Farm

As the next two years passed along, another son Don Haynes was born while James was serving in World War II, in the Mediterranean Sea area with the Navy. Thelma continued to be provided shelter for herself and the babies with Nell, James' sister Clio and James' father in the College Park, GA neighborhoods.

Later a sister **Nancy was born** and she was the apple of her daddy's eye. In time the family moved to northeast Georgia near Lavonia and they **settled on a small farm. Afterwards they acquired twelve dairy cows** and twice every day James, Jim, and Don milked the cows by hand. In time they added more cows and modernized their operations with milking machines. But, it still meant that **Jim and Don had to milk the cows every morning before going to school and** every afternoon after returning home.

About the time that Jim was ten years old, another baby joined their family. His brother **Joel was Jim's tag-a-long, with Jim responsible for tending to many of Joel's basic needs**, including diaper changing and such. Their **mother worked at the local sewing plant so that they could have food on the table.**

A few years later, the family farm had to be sold for economic reasons and they moved in to town to live in a small house in

Lavonia, GA. James and his brother Sam worked on the building of the dam at Lake Hartwell on the Savannah River that separated the states of Georgia and South Carolina. Once that project was completed, James and Sam traveled to Kansas to work as carpenters on the building of the missile silos for the Defense System of the United States Government.

All of this left Thelma home alone with four children to raise. She **depended heavily on Jim** to help her with the other three children and he carried responsibilities way beyond those of his years.

While in high school, Jim worked on the weekends at a turkey farm. It was a job that he did not like because of the terrible odors on the farm from the turkeys and the bad habits of the turkeys, with their pecking at him. Later he was able to work at the drug store in town with its old-fashioned soda fountain, where he served soda drinks and other delicious treats.

Off into the Wild Blue Yonder with the Air Force

Although Jim wanted to further his education after high school, it was out of the question. So, he joined the Air Force and served a four-year tour of duty. His training was in the field of teletype repair work. He was stationed at Ramey Air Force Base, in Puerto Rico. While in Puerto Rico, he was placed not far from Cuba. It was at the time of the **Bay of Pigs invasion. It was a scary time** for a young man just starting his tour with the Air Force. Meanwhile, the Russians were in a threatening position ready to strike the United States!

A College Education

After completing his tour of duty with the Air Force, Jim attended Georgia State University in Atlanta and earned a Bachelor of Business degree in Accounting in 1970. Having been out of the study mode for five years, it was a challenge to get back into the groove of study.

During the college years, Jim worked part time at night and went to school full time during the day. Bette did just the opposite as she completed her Master's degree at Georgia State at night.

Jim's career

Graduating with a degree in accounting, Jim ventured out on a different path than Bette. He was more interested in **Corporate Accounting. As a result, his career was more focused on positions in the financial management of a company. Jim held various corporate controller positions in different types of corporations.**

Later Jim became interested in computer installations and had his **own business that offered consulting services**. He then specialized his services, installing computer systems for flower shops all around the United States. He enjoyed working with the many different shop owners and traveling extensively throughout the eastern part of the country. Eventually competition from grocery store florists brought that business to an end.

In his last years of work, Jim obtained his life and health insurance licenses to sell related insurance products in Georgia.

Prison Ministry

As a result of his involvement with **Walk to Emmaus**, Jim became interested in volunteering to be a member of **Kairos Prison Ministry** in the prison system of Georgia. This was one of the most rewarding activities that Jim undertook with his life. Just as Jim has ministered to the prisoners, they have ministered to him. **Prison Ministry has been a natural extension of his parents' work**. His father James worked for the Florida prison system, as a construction foreman, in the Ocala, Florida area with prisoners who did construction work. His mother Thelma worked in the Ocala area as a corrections officer in a women's prison.

Three Special Aunts

Jim's life was surrounded by **love and support from three of James' sisters... Nell, Clio, and Ruth.** The support was there in physical, emotional, and spiritual ways. That support continued from each of those three wonderful ladies until the day that each of them died. They were an integral part of the spiritual life that Jim brought to our marriage. You will learn more about them in this book. It was my privilege to know Aunt Clio and Aunt Ruth for many years in the beginning years of our marriage. They took care of our children Janet and Ricky for us so that I was able to work and attend graduate school. They **treated Jim and me just like we were their own children and our children were their own grandchildren.** We were totally blessed to have them as part of our extended family as well as our spiritual family.

Humble Beginnings Forward

As I have written this summary of Jim's life, I have viewed it in a somewhat different light than I normally do. Before beginning to write, we sat down and I asked Jim a lot of questions. There were many things that I had forgotten about from his humble beginnings.

> If it had not been for **certain relatives**, there would have been **no inn for the family to stay in, nor any food** for the babies.

> The aunts who watched over him and taught him God's ways and love, provided him with the **sweet and gentle spirit that guide his daily walk.**

As you read the story "Lemons at the Beach", of how Jim and I met and how he proposed to me, you will understand the spiritual basis that he brought to our **God-ordained marriage**.

As I share with you some of the challenges that we have faced as a family, I know that the **humble beginnings from which he came and the love he was surrounded with, have been the solid rock** upon which we have stood, **NOT** sinking sand!

Thelma, Jim's mother, with Jim (7 yrs.), Nancy (3yrs), and Don(5 yrs.) d. in Lavonia, GA 1949.

The Parable of the Two Builders

One of the parables in the New Testament illustrates that point very well.

"Therefore whoever hears these sayings of Mine, and does them, I will liken him to a wise man who built his house on the rock: and the rain descended, the floods came, and the winds blew, and beat on that house; and it did not fall, for it was founded on the rock.

But everyone who hears these sayings of Mine, and does not do them, will be like a foolish man who built his house on the sand; and the rain descended, the floods came, and the winds blew and beat on that house; and it fell. And great was its fall." Matthew 7:24-27 NKJV

Baby Jim with curly hair.

Baby Bette with stuffed animal doggie.

Jim, Don (d), Nancy, Joel on John Deere tractor – full-sized
on family farm in Lavonia, GA 1951. As usual, Jim was placed
in charge, even with a dangerous ride on the tractor.

All four kids, sitting along side the dirt road
by the family farm in Lavonia, GA

2 men fishing. Pop Haynes (grandpa) and Uncle
Frank Haynes (d) Thelma's father and brother
fishing at the St. John's River, FL 4/24/59

Thelma and siblings Hattie Lee Edwards (d), Frank Haynes
(d), Dorene Cline (d), Thelma (d), Ruby Stith (d)

Aunt Clio Mabry, Jim's father's sister. Provider of care and support for the family and a strong Christian supporting role model for all of the family.

Aunt Nell Mabry, another one of Jim's father's sisters. Also a provider for the family's needs on and off the farm, as well as their spiritual needs. She died at an early age on a Christmas Day. 4/7/29.

The only Christmas that all of Jim's siblings and parents
spent Christmas together. Jim, Don (d), Joel, Nancy.

The only Christmas that all of Jim's siblings and
their children spent Christmas with their parents
Ma and PaPa. 1983 at Jim and Bette's house.

CHAPTER 5

Our Children and Theirs

When Jim and I were engaged, he jokingly told me that he wanted to **continue the traditions of his mother's and father's families and have lots of children. In Southern terms, that meant keeping me "pregnant and barefooted."** Now "barefooted I didn't mind, because I seldom wore shoes in the house. However, I wasn't sure that I was up to having seven or eight children, as was the history in his parents' backgrounds.

Janet Elaine was our first child to be born, arriving in June 1970, shortly after our graduations from Georgia State University and my passing the last section of the CPA exam. We were thrilled and surprised to have a girl. Jim had said that there was no way for us to have a "girl" given his family history. But, God had other plans for us!

After graduating from Emory University with a Bachelor's degree in Religion and Sociology, she **married her college sweetheart Chris Kenney and later they had a son Andrew**. At the age of twenty-nine, **Janet became a widow** and raised her son Andrew on her own. More of her story is in the book.

Richard "Ricky" James was our second child, joining our family in May 1972. Much different than Janet, Ricky was artistic and creative. He loved the outdoors and exploring nature. We were stunned when we realized that he had difficulty with reading and that school work was a much different challenge for him than for Janet. As parents, we had to **learn different parenting skills.**

Getting Ricky to **accept his God-given artistic talents was a monumental task for us.** Today he is a very successful graphic artist, who has also matured with managerial skills. His work includes managing printing presses that are capable of printing in ten colors on a job at one time.

The light of his world is his daughter Jewel, who enjoyed riding horses and competing in barrel and pole racing competition, while in high school. They also spend time with their other horses, fishing, doing archery, and hunting together. A far cry from the artistic world, it is neat to see a son who has developed in so many different ways. Today Jewel is pursuing a degree in pharmacy studies.

Richard is married to the former **Jeri Regina White**, who had a daughter **Miranda McEachern** who was a couple years old when Jeri and Richard married. Jeri had been interested in horses for a long time and it was her interest in them that got Jewel involved in horse competition racing.

Over the years, Jeri has had to deal with her own health problems, which has limited some of her activities from what she would like to do. For the most part, she has worked as a 9-1-1 or EMT operator. Her assertive and inquisitive personality makes her an excellent employee for this type work. For many years, she home schooled Jewel, at which Jewel excelled.

Miranda has always had a heart for children with disabilities or life-long infirmities. After doing an internship at Disney World in

Orlando, while attending Georgia Southern University, Miranda is now working with a non-profit organization that serves such children and their families. Hearts of compassion are at work in this family unit. Jeri has been fully devoted to her role of motherhood in raising Jewel, her and Richard's baby.

Cynthia Joy was God's unexpected gift to us in April 1980. The pregnancy was surrounded in unhealthy circumstances and we were **forced to deal with the issue of abortion**. That decision is one of the stories later in this book.

Cynthia's life has been complicated by many medical issues, including heart ablation surgery at the age of thirteen. Our faith was tried many times over with episodes of anaphylactic shock. She gave birth to two daughters Kaley and Abby after complicated pregnancies.

Six years ago, at the age of thirty-three, Cynthia suffered her very first grand mal seizure and was later **diagnosed with epilepsy and stress related seizures**. Because of the number of daily seizures and their severity, she had to move in with Jim and me. She is not able to drive or work, or live independently. More of her stories are included in both books, including **surprise twists about the epilepsy.**

The well-known minister and author Dr. Rev. Charles Stanley wrote the book "How to Keep Your Kids on Your Team." The book opens with a discussion about our **children being a GIFT from God**. That was probably one of the most important books I ever read as a parent. Those words have never left my heart or actions with my children or grandchildren. No matter where or what we have faced, I have tried to remember that they are all God's gift and I have tried to handle life's events accordingly for each of those **precious gifts**.

A few verses from the Book of Psalms address this very concept of children being a gift from the Lord. And, as a grandma, I love Psalm 128:6, as I am sure other **grandparents** do so also.

> Children are a gift from the LORD;
> They are a reward from Him.
> Children born to a young man

are like sharp arrows in a warrior's hands.
How happy is the man whose quiver is full of them!

Psalm 127:3-5 NLT

within your home.

And look at all those children!
They all sit He will not be put to shame when he
confronts his accusers at the city gates.

Psalm 127:3-5 NLT

3. Your wife will be like a fruitful vine,
Flourishing around your table
As vigorous and healthy as young olive trees.

4. That is the LORD's reward
For those who fear Him.

May you live to enjoy your grandchildren?

Psalm 128: 3-4, 6 NLT

Upclose view of all four kids on John Deere tractor, with Jim being placed in charge of this dangerous undertaking.

Janet at approx. age 3. Very petite in size, she and Ricky
were about the same size at this time. Her dress was made
by Aunt Ruth, who took care of her, while Bette worked.
Aunt Ruth was one of Aunt Clio's sisters. August 1973.

Ricky was approx. 18 months old. Little towheads, he and
Janet both had blond hair. He loved playing with keys.

Ricky is holding his baby Jewel, relaxing at home
while holding her at five months 7/10/2000.

Jeri, Richard Mabry's wife and Jewel's mom. Life
of the party. Family holiday meal time 12/25/01,
always a time of fun and wild entertainment.

Grandma Haley, age 80, holding Cynthia, age 9 months at
her infant baptism at Hopewell UMC. The two conversed
on the phone until Grandma was 99 years old.

Rev. Bob Partridge holding Cynthia, whom he had just baptized
at Hopewell UMC. He was instrumental in preserving her life
in the story about the decision surrounding abortion, in the
story, "Testing our Values." He is also one of the characters
in the horse accident and Prayers of Thanksgiving stories.

Four generations gathered together for Cynthia's baptism. Bette Conklin Mabry, Lorraine Haley Conklin (d), Elizabeth Haley (d), baby Cynthia Joy

With a pretty smile, Janet's second college graduation number 2 from Georgia State University in Atlanta, GA earning a degree in Community Counseling in 1996.

Jim, a proud father, walking his beautiful daughter Janet down the aisle at her wedding to Chris Kenney6/27/97 at Fayetteville UMC.

Janet, a toddler trying on Mimi's (grandma Lorraine Conklin) mink stole she received for Christmas 12/25/69.

Vacation time at DeSoto State Park in northeast Alabama, including climbing on huge rugged boulder rocks and a trip afterwards to nearby Ft. Payne, AL, home of the acclaimed singing group Alabama. One of many vacations spent with cousin Gary Finzer, son of Lois Finzer. Ricky has on his favorite white hat from Myrtle Beach, SC.

Our furry friend Snoopy, a pug, age 14, dressed in one of Kaley's
favorite dresses, which had a watermelon pattern. His antics
are special to the family, including taking care of Bette.

Cynthia, standing in front of lavender and blue hydrangea
bushes, which are summer time favorites.

CHAPTER 6

Lemons at the Beach

"For I know the plans I have for you."
Jeremiah 29:11 NASB

Spring Break

The last few months had been completely different than I had expected. A junior in college at Case Western Reserve University in Cleveland, Ohio, I had **come home to Florida for Spring break**. My sister Lois and I decided to go to Cocoa Beach on Monday afternoon to enjoy one of our favorite things to do – swim and hang out at the beach.

Our daddy worked with the Space Program near the beach area where we were going. At that time most families had only one vehicle and that meant we had to take Daddy back to work after lunch; stay at the beach for the entire afternoon; and then pick him up at the end of the work day.

Cocoa Beach

We were headed for the area of Cocoa Beach where you drive down to the central area of the beach area itself. We entered through the green gated area where the sand was solid. That meant you could actually drive down onto the beach, park your car, set up your area, and enjoy the day. Since the sand wasn't soft you didn't have to worry about spinning your wheels and getting stuck up to the floorboards in the sand. And, there were **those who did lots of cruising on the beach – guys and girls! However, since it was a Monday, we didn't expect to see much cruising activity.**

Cocoa Beach was a wonderful place to swim because of the way the Gulf Stream currents warmed and protected the sugar white sandy beach. The waves were of the friendly sort, but on occasion the surfers enjoyed riding the higher waves. The edge of the shoreline provided a pleasant place to walk or run, which we also enjoyed doing. It was a common site to see children playing in the sand as they built sand castles or covered their friends in the sand. Even adults joined in the fun. Games of Frisbee or catch were common. People walked their dogs on the beach and played ball with them. The beach area was just down the street from the well-known Ron Jon shop, which later grew into a huge retail establishment. However, since this was in 1965, the area was very sleepy and small beach type homes existed in the area instead.

My sister, who was two years younger and attended the same college and I set up our blanket and got ready for an afternoon of swimming. Since it was the first week in April, the temperatures were pleasantly warm in the 80's, with cool breezes. The hot summer time had not hit the area yet.

A while later a **car of guys parked close by**. They were from Patrick Air Force Base, which was located between Cocoa Beach and Satellite Beach where we lived. As was our routine, Lois and I **got out our lemons to squeeze on our hair** to lighten our light brown hair. Yes…that was what we did in those days…used lemons on our hair! That was what the guys needed to use to start a conversation with us. Lemons! **When was the last time you started a conversation over a lemon,** unless it was a car?

A Week of Dates

Most of the afternoon, in between swimming and walking on the beach, Lois spent time talking with Jim, and I talked with Bob, although there were others that we talked with. The time passed quickly and soon it was time to leave.

Much to our surprise, Jim and Bob asked Lois and me out for a date that evening. When we told our parents about that, **the phone rang, with the guys confirming the time of the date.** So much for Daddy's words! He was going to have to eat them! It was a **miracle that we were allowed to go out with men from the Air Force that we knew nothing about!** Maybe it had something to do with the fact that both our parents worked with the military on a daily basis with the Space Program. It cost the guys twenty-five cents to take us to the drive-in movie to see the "Americanization of Emily" starring Julie Andrews.

When we got ready to get into the car, **I asked Jim "who is driving?"** even though I knew he had been driving the shiny black Dodge at the beach. Being the older sister, I quickly told my younger sister, "Lois, you can get in the back seat with Bob and I'll get in the front seat with Jim." I had made my mind up earlier in the day that I wanted to go out with Jim. Little did I know what plans God had in mind for me. **I didn't even realize that God had plans for His children!** The rest of the week passed quickly with Jim and I seeing each other just about every day.

When I returned to my dorm, **I told my roommate Louise, "I am going to marry Jim."** Now, how did I know that after a week?

I had barely dated anyone in the past. What did I know about Jim? What did I know about married life? What would I know about living with someone else? I knew that Louise was getting married in July and I was going to be in her wedding. I knew that it was springtime and the campus in Cleveland was so romantic with all of the flowers. A campus environment is a place filled with romantic relationships.

After returning to Cleveland from the exciting Spring break, Jim and I wrote to each other three or four times a week. Phone calls were few and far between. In 1965, phone calls were made using pay phones that you placed coins into the slots for so many minutes of talking time. The first minute for a call from Atlanta to Cleveland after 7 pm on a Sunday, cost a quarter, which was a lot of money in those days. Every day at lunchtime, I hurried to the front desk of the dorm **to see if there was a letter from Jim.**

Does Anything Good Ever Come Out of "Mono"?

Earlier in the school year, I had to withdraw from my classes and return to my home in Florida, because I became very ill with mono. I was only able to complete two of my five courses with special arrangements from the college. What was amazing was that **I completed my first accounting course on my own and earned an A in that course.** It was at that point that I recognized my interest and abilities in the field of accounting. Since it was the middle of my junior year, I was able to **declare a major in Economics and a minor in Accounting and if I took one course in summer school, I would still be able to graduate with my class.**

So, that summer I took a Psychology class from Rollins College at their extension campus at Patrick Air Force Base, where Jim was stationed. How convenient was that! We had a break during the three-hour class and **Jim and I always met during the break time.** And then he would drive me home, after classes were over in the evening. Our relationship grew and we were very happy together.

A Very Strange Proposal

The end of June arrived and it was **time for Jim's discharge from the Air Force.** He would be leaving the area and moving to Atlanta. Jim took me back to the place where we had first met at Cocoa Beach. It was a beautiful summer night, with the moon shining down on the Atlantic Ocean. The waves shimmered in the moonlight and the sound of the waves lapping on the shore was soothing as we took in the magic of the evening and the reality of his impending departure.

Then, Jim proposed, asking me to marry him. However, he told me that **God would always be first in his life.** Talk about bursting someone's bubble! That sent me into a tailspin!!!! I didn't understand. I didn't like him saying that to me. I was young, naïve, and in love. Madly in love. How could he love anyone more than me??? I was selfish and wanted to be first. Basically, I was hurt. But, I couldn't let him know that. I wanted to marry him more than anything else, so I had to be a big girl and put all those thoughts aside. I accepted his proposal, but I knew there were conditions attached to his proposal. **I had a challenge to face that was foreign to me and I was going to have to do something about it.**

Clearly, God had given me the **gift of a Godly man**, but at the time I did not understand that concept or the significance of that gift in my life's journey. It wasn't until **many years later that I understood the full significance of God's gift to me.**

> "For I know the plans that I have for you," declares the LORD. "plans for welfare and not for calamity to give you a future and a hope. Then you will call upon Me and come and pray to Me, and I will listen to you. You will seek Me and find Me when you search for Me with all your heart." Jeremiah 29:11-13 NASB

Back to Jim's proposal to me.

I had very strong opinions about college education and degrees. When he proposed, I countered to him and said that I would have to return for my senior year of college and graduate before getting married. In other words, **I was not interested in dropping out right now**. I had seen too many of my classmates do that. Also, he would have to promise to start college or have plans in place to do so by the time we got married.

I find it interesting that I have never seen or heard of either one of these discussions taking place at the time of any other marriage proposal. Usually, it is a "yes" or "let's think about it"; not two serious conditions being discussed immediately, becoming part of the **"covenants" between the intended parties**. As I look back on our relationship, the **scary part is how little we knew about each other.** However, we did share the same values in life, spiritual beliefs, family values, and goals.

> "Trust in the Lord with all your heart,
> And lean not on your own understanding;
> In all your ways acknowledge Him,
> And He shall direct your paths." Prov.3:5-6 NKJV

The Sunday before Jim was to be discharged from the Air Force and leave Patrick Air Force Base, he spent the day with my family. My daddy always watched Bonanza on Sunday night TV. However, that Sunday night, the watching of Bonanza was delayed when Jim asked my father for permission to marry me, along with my mother's permission. They really weren't too surprised, since Jim had taken me to meet his parents the weekend before. Also, Jim had attended church with me at our newly organized church and that was important to them.

Faith, commitment, and perseverance

We married a year later on August 6^{th, 1966} at the United Methodist Church in Satellite Beach, Florida. This next August we will be celebrating our 54th anniversary. If it were not for our faith and commitment to the Lord, we probably would not have persevered. We are also thankful for the love and support of friends and family who have been there for us, **comforting us through the years as we have traveled our journey as husband and wife.** Their comforting ways have **helped us rise above** the circumstances of life.

> "Through love serve one another....You shall love your neighbor as yourself." Gal 5:13-14 NKJV

> "Bear one another's burdens and so fulfill the Law of Christ." Gal 6:2 NKJV

> "And let us not grow weary while doing good, for in due season, we shall reap if we do not lose heart. Therefore, as we have opportunity, let us do good to all, especially to those who are of the household of faith." Gal 6:9-10 NKJV

Jim and Bette after saying wedding vows.

Jim and Bette cutting wedding cake. Table cloth is a family heirloom used by Bette, Lois, Janet, and Cynthia. Also used at Jim and Bette's 50th wedding anniversary celebration.

CHAPTER 7

Grandma and Gramps Conklin

<u>The Big White House</u>

Some of my earliest memories are those of living with my daddy's parents, Grandma and Gramps C (or Conklin.) We lived in a large, white two story house that was built in 1845. It was known as the Haynes house, which is interesting, because Jim's mother's maiden name was Haynes. It is now listed on an Ohio State Historical Register.

The house was divided equally by a staircase from the second floor to the main floor of the house. **I spent much of my time over on my grandparents' side,** helping Grandma with her daily chores and activities, from the age of three until eight, when we moved to another house.

The house was located on a corner lot, facing the main street of the small suburban town of Poland, Ohio, outside of Youngstown, Ohio. A block away from the house was the Methodist Church that we attended. A few more blocks away were Johnson's Hardware, Seidel's Market – a small grocery, the fire station and a few other businesses all on our side of the street. The library was on the second floor of the fire station and we walked several blocks from the school to the library for library time. That was always one of my favorite times of the school schedule—going to the library.

On the other side of the street were Poland Home Bakery, Barnes drug store, Islay's dairy, Dr. Vance's, the beauty shop, and the Presbyterian Church. Just past those businesses was a bridge that crossed Yellow Creek and then a rise up the hill. A turn to the left on the next street brought you to Poland Union, the elementary school Lois and I attended.

Even after we moved away from Ohio, I remained close to Grandma via letter writing. Gramps would add to her writing, which was an absolute treat, because of his dry humor. When we lived in Florida and after they moved to Florida, I would spend weeks at a time with them during the summer months. **Lois and I have felt that we were blessed to have had those times with Grandma and Gramps.** Now that we are acquainted with all of our adult cousins, it is a privilege to be able to share with them about our times of living with our grandparents and the summer visits.

Lois and Gramps had a special bond when it came to telling stories and using their imaginations. There was a green "kitty-cat" that was a friend with Lois and Gramps. It lived under the cushions on the sofa in Grandma and Grandpa's living room. **That kitty-cat brought "comfort and compassion" to Lois** in a special way without those words ever being used. The kitty-cat wasn't part of my world, just Lois's. I think that was really important, because Lois needed her own comfort creatures, just as you and I do.

Needles and Thread

Since I was two years older than Lois, I spent more time with Grandma with the sewing projects than Lois did. I would help with lifting the pressure foot up and down on the sewing machine for Grandma. Some days she would give me the big tin cake box that had all the buttons in it. She would give me a big needle and heavy thread to string the buttons on. **I would sit for hours at a time amusing myself, while exclaiming over all the pretty buttons. At five years of age, I thought that I was really something!**

In those days, people would darn the holes in their socks to extend the life of them. Grandma would give me a big needle and thread to darn Gramps' socks. **I would "fix" them by sewing them into a big wad of fabric. There was no way that Gramps would be able to put his foot into the sock once I was through with it. Grandma never said anything to me.** She just took them apart later in the day after I went back to our side of the house.

Grandma sewed clothes for both Lois and me. However, **she stretched the rules about look-alike or twin clothes**. She would make the outfits in different colors for each of us or at times even a different pattern, which would irritate our mom. **Lois and I were just happy to have new clothes!** Grandma would let us help her as much as she could with the sewing of each new outfit. I remember little red plaid jumpers and the yellow dress with box pleats in the skirt section. Mom really disliked that outfit, but I loved the sassy skirt and bright yellow material. It is still vivid in my memory. I always wanted to wear that outfit, much to her dismay. Poor Grandma, Mom would pitch fits! The clothes Grandma sewed didn't look like the pink dotted Swiss ones Mom would sew.

All of this helped to instill an interest in sewing that was very important for me in later years. In about tenth grade I started babysitting and earning money that I used to purchase fabric and supplies to sew my own clothes. I made all of my skirts, pants, tops, shorts, and night clothes (pj's.) By the time I was in college I was sewing woolen suits, fancy blouses, jackets, and formal dresses.

I **even sewed my wedding dress** when Jim and I married. For many years afterwards, until the stores started carrying petite sized clothes, I made most of my clothes, including professionally designed suits. **Grandma's loving compassionate ways prepared me** to want to do this craft that required patience and logical thinking. Of course, Mom had to censor all of my sewing, even though I paid for the materials with my baby sitting money. Most of that money was earned by babysitting for a family of seven children, being paid at the rate of fifty cents an hour.

Grandma's Food Allergies

Grandma was allergic to some foods which made it difficult for eating. She was **allergic to wheat, tomatoes, and apples**. She couldn't even touch a tomato. Amazingly, she baked every week, even though she couldn't eat the baked goods! She made pies, cookies, and cakes. At Christmas time, there were all kinds of cookies. Lois and I helped with decorating and icing all of them. It was **one of the highlights of the year**. There were Santa's, snowmen, gingerbread men, Christmas tree balls, candles, and other designs.

During the Depression, she baked pies and other baked goods to help earn money for the family's expenses. I can't even begin to **imagine spending time baking and not being able to taste** and savor the delicious morsels of crumbs.

We were always aware of the foods she couldn't eat like spaghetti, sliced tomatoes, apples, apple sauce, white bread, and cookies. It was difficult for us to understand the concept of someone being allergic to food types. **Lois and I learned about compassion for our grandmother at an early age**, with respect to this aspect of her health issues. While I was **learning to have compassion for her and to not make fun of her,** I had no idea that I was also learning the lessons for myself.

When I was about thirty-five years old, my body became very allergic to a lot of foods. For several years, I was very limited as to what I could eat. I was always fixing two meals at a time; one for my family and one for myself. Part of what helped me get through this time was the fact that I had learned to comfort my grandma in my little girl ways, as a young child and then be compassionate with her needs when I was older. **God had prepared me in advance to be able to deal with my own problem,** by giving me the opportunity to show comfort and compassion in a Christ-like manner, ahead of time, to a very special person in my life.

Flowers and Veggies

Gramps claim to fame was gardening, both vegetables and flowers. Until the time that he died, he always had some type of flowers (unique or domestic) that he tended to on a regular basis. He also instilled that interest in my father. **I never see a Pansy or Violet that I don't think of** the small flower garden that was close to the back porch. I remember the zinnias, the gladiolas, the hollyhocks, the marigolds, and all the other flowers in the huge garden of flowers. The rose bushes were favorites. When they moved to Florida, he learned to raise poinsettias, crotons, lilies, oleanders, and other native tropical plants.

The vegetable garden provided food for the winter time and fresh vegetables for the summer time. I think he raised just about everything possible in that garden, except Southern vegetables like okra and yellow squash. Grandma spent much time canning the harvest from the garden. I think everyone's favorite though was the red raspberry patch, (located by the old wooden barn), which served as the garage for our cars. Lois and I used to sneak into the patch and **fill our tummies with juicy, ripe berries**. Then when Gramps would ask us who had been in the raspberry patch, we would be guilty! We always looked forward to bowls of raspberries and sugar or milk, sitting at the table eating with Grandma and Gramps, doing our thing.

The flowers provided an added bonus time for Lois and me. We **learned about flower arranging**, since Grandma kept fresh flowers, from the garden, on the dining room table. We talked about the "little faces" of the pansies and violets and made up stories about them. We learned to appreciate the beauty of God's creation.

Get me to the Church on Time

There is no doubt in my mind what **Grandma's legacy** was to me. Lois will tell you the same answer. Many of my first cousins will tell you the same answer. She was **our spiritual mentor, our guide to being a Christian, our example.** Moses, M-0-S-E-S to her grandchildren. Without her, Lois and I would have never known our Lord as intimately as we did, at such an early age! It just happened naturally!

Every day I observed Grandma and Gramps read the "Upper Room", a devotional booklet that is provided by the Methodist Church to its members. They read it before their breakfast or lunch time meal. **Grandma read her Bible regularly and I was no stranger to watching her do those things**. Often times she read it in the early afternoons, in conjunction with her nap time. Our grandparents prayed together before their meal times. During these years, Christian books were not available to the general public like they are today. A few years ago, my cousin **Libby gave me Grandma's Bible that she read daily.** I cherish having that Bible in my library of books, especially, since it brings back so many precious memories.

Even though the church was only a block away from our house in Poland, Grandma and Gramps saw to it that we were walked there safely, every week to attend Sunday school. Later we would sit with Grandma during the church service, while Gramps served as an usher.

Until the time that she died, Grandma was one of my Christian spiritual mentors. **She never wavered in her faith.** I knew who

Jesus was because of her. Other people knew about being a Christian because of Grandma.

It wasn't until recently, after my mom died, that I learned about some of the gifts that were given to Grandma in appreciation of her service for the Lord. She was given a **quilt that was handmade back in 1857, in Scotland, with the women's signatures hand engraved on it.** That quilt is now mine and I cherish it because of the significance it represents. Recently I passed this quilt on to one of my granddaughters, Jewel for her future safekeeping.

"Let the children come to me. Don't stop them! For the Kingdom of God belongs to such as these. I assure you, anyone who doesn't have their kind of faith will never get into the Kingdom of God." Then He took the children into his arms and placed His hands on their heads and blessed them. Mark 10:14-16 NLT

Death as a Journey

When my mom's father died, I was home from college, sick with mono. Grandpa Haley was to be taken back to Ohio for burial from Mom's place in Florida. It had been a traumatic experience, seeing Grandpa pass away in front of me at my parents' home. Since I was not well enough to travel because of the mono, Grandma and Gramps Conklin had me stay with them while all the others traveled to Ohio from Florida.

It was **my first major experience with death**, and Grandma was the best person to be with. She explained to me that **death was the next "journey" she was looking forward to, in her life and that I should not fear it. Somehow, her words provided the comfort that I needed** and I have never forgotten them. In fact, I have shared this story with others many times.

"For we know that when this earthly tent we live in is taken down—when we die and leave these bodies—we will have a home in Heaven, an eternal body made for us by God himself and not by human hands. We grow weary in our present bodies, and we long for the day when we will put on our heavenly bodies like new clothing. For we will not be spirits without bodies, but we will put on new heavenly bodies." 2 Corinthians 5:1-3 NLT

A Humble Life

Grandma and Gramps lived a modest life, interspersed with years of living in poor conditions. They moved about during the years before and during the Depression as Gramps tried his best to be employed. They moved from Ohio to the Plains states and then lived several places in Colorado. When they returned to Ohio, the **family had to be separated with the children being placed with other family members until they could be financially stable**. During this time my daddy had rheumatic fever and they were not able to provide him with proper medical care. This resulted in permanent heart damage for him and eventually led to his early death at age fifty-five.

"That is why we never give up. Though our bodies are dying, our spirits are being renewed every day. For our present troubles are quite small and won't last very long. Yet they produce for us an immeasurably great glory that will last forever! So we don't look at the troubles we can see right now; rather, we look forward to what we have not yet seen. For the troubles we see will soon be over, but the joys to come will last forever." 2Corinthians 4:16-18 NLT

Grandma's Health

For most of her adult life, Grandma was not well. Unfortunately, modern medicine was not available to her. Even in today's world, medicine probably would not be able to address all of her needs. Apparently, she is the person from whom Lois and I have inherited the **genes for autoimmune diseases**, as well as our daughters and other members in the family tree. To me, she was an amazing woman, doing what she could when she was able, always doing for others. **She is one of my heroes!** One of my mentors! One of my guides!

Something would always rub me the wrong way, when people would criticize Grandma for needing to rest or being sickly. Or they would talk about her "spells." Or the length of time for her to get over a hospital stay. Personally, **I feel nothing but compassion for her**, since I have the autoimmune diseases that I have. I feel that she was not diagnosed properly, because of the lack of medical knowledge and limited testing capabilities. We may share some of the same illnesses and then <u>again</u> we may have cousin illnesses. It doesn't matter. She did the best she could with **the invisible illnesses**. She was filled with courage.

"Our dying bodies make us groan and sigh, but it's not that we want to die and have no bodies at all. We want to slip into our new bodies so that these dying bodies will be swallowed up by everlasting life. God himself has prepared us for this, and as a guarantee he has given us his Holy Spirit." 2Corinthians 5:4–5 NLT

"So we are always confident, even though we know that as long as we live in these bodies, we are not at home with the LORD. That is why we live by believing and not by seeing." 2Corinthians 5:6-7 NLT

A Mother's Sacrifice

Grandma and Gramps had three children, including their oldest child, Caroline Ruth who married Lawrence Robinson, a former member of the Mormon faith. Ruth became a registered Nurse and her husband entered seminary to become a minister of the Methodist faith. In the late 1940's, they answered the call to **become missionaries and were assigned to the Belgian Congo**.

"This is the wonderful message he has given us to tell others. We are Christ's ambassadors..." 2Corinthians 5:19b-20 NLT

Aunt Ruth and Uncle Lawrence served in the Congo from 1949 on into the 1960's in various capacities. They raised their five children there, with them attending several of the boarding schools in the larger Congolese cities. Ruth's youngest two children were born in the Congo and one of them still works there, as does one of his sons, who graduated from an American college several years ago.

Because of Ruth's missionary service, Grandma became very interested in missionary work and supported their efforts. In some of the papers that I recently inherited, I found a letter that Grandma wrote, explaining her feelings about Ruth and her family being in an underdeveloped and unsafe environment. Grandma expressed her concern for her grandchildren's health and educational needs. In those days, they traveled from the US to the Congo by way of New York City's harbors. The boats they sailed on probably were not the safest. Grandma apparently **carried her concerns to women's missionary support groups within the Methodist church,** creating awareness of the conditions under which the missionaries and their families served.

As a teen-ager and later as a college student, I remember that every time we went to see Grandma and Gramps, Daddy would check to see if there were **any new aero-grams** (a special air mail letter) from his sister Ruth. They were the one form of communication used, unless there was an extreme emergency and then a telegram or ham radio message would be the form of communication. The aero-grams would be typewritten to take advantage of as much space as possible. They would be filled with detailed information about the mission work, as well as personal news. Additionally, updates about the political and government turmoil would complete the newsletters.

It was also important that Mom and Daddy be kept updated about all of Ruth and her family's comings and goings for very specific reasons. In the event that the children had to be evacuated for any reason from the Congo, they were to be sent to live with our family. It was an **awesome responsibility lurking in the shadows at all times.** Although the need to care for the Robinson children never arose, they were always in our hearts and concerns. Their daughter

Libby did come and live with us for several summers while she was attending college. To this day, she is a sister to Lois and me!

Grandma made it her duty to keep other family members and churches updated on her daughter Ruth's needs, as Ruth served the Lord. She certainly was involved in the role of being a Comforter for Aunt Ruth and family. She had a sense of what their needs were, without being told. Perhaps some of that was a natural result of Grandma's own environment in which she grew up. Personally, I learned much about concern and compassion for people serving in the difficult roles of mission work from observing my grandparents in their support role with their daughter and her family. I also became **aware of the plight of the people** who live in countries like the Congo and feel a sense of compassion that I would not feel otherwise.

One of the most difficult situations for Grandma was when Gramps died and Aunt Ruth was in Congo. Naturally, Grandma wanted Ruth to be notified quickly. Fortunately, we were able to **find a ham operator** who was able to make a good connection to the Congo and the message was conveyed. This time someone else was comforting Grandma. And so, the **principles of sharing God's comforting Grace were working full circle!**

As I have studied the Book of Acts and the apostle Paul's travels, there have been many times that I have thought about making **comparisons with Paul and the other Biblical characters with Grandma and Aunt Ruth**. Furthermore, Paul's letters to the various churches prompt me to think of the challenges facing Ruth and Lawrence as they served in the Congo and later as they served in many challenging assignments in the United States. Certainly the concept of Compassion and God's Comforting Grace are absolute necessities in these roles and situations.

Through my grandparents' obedience to the Lord, these graces were part of Ruth's life. She was then able to take them to those that she was called upon to serve in the roles of nursing and mission work. Later in life Ruth devoted much of her efforts to Social Justice Issues within the United Methodist Church, until the time of her death in her eighties.

In Paul's writings near the end of his life, when he was imprisoned in Rome for the second time, he wrote the following to his beloved friend Timothy.

"I have been reminded of your sincere faith, which first lived in your grandmother Lois and in your mother Eunice and, I am persuaded, now lives in you also. For this reason I remind you to fan into flame the gift of God, which is in you through the laying on of my hands. For God did not give us a spirit of timidity, but a spirit of power, of love, and of self-discipline." 2Timothy 1:5-7 NIV

I believe that Paul's admonition regarding the Scriptures was an important part of Grandma's life and accordingly strongly influenced her children's and grandchildren's lives, as well as others in the community at large.

"All Scripture is God-breathed and is useful for teaching, rebuking, correcting and training in righteousness, so that the man of God may be thoroughly equipped for every good work." 2 Timothy 3:16-17 NIV

A Special Love

There is no doubt that my life, the earthly and the spiritual, has been strongly influenced by my Grandma and Gramps Conklin. It was through my everyday experiences with Grandma that I learned about being comforted and shown compassion. She was the one who introduced me to mercurochrome bunnies being painted on my "boo-boo's" when I fell and scraped my knees. She wiped my tears away with her apron—she wore one most of the day every day, covering her dress.

In many ways I didn't fully appreciate my grandparents until later in life, but that is the way it is with many things in our lives. Recently, I have learned of her influence and comforting ways that she shared with my cousins in her later years. After Gramps died, she moved to California to be with Ruth and her son George's families.

At that point, other members of the family had the opportunity to experience her love and compassion.

Clearly, Grandma lived a life that reflected holiness as defined in Peter's letter to the scattered Christians.

"So think clearly and exercise self-control. Look forward to the special blessings that will come to you at the return of Jesus Christ. Obey God because you are His children. Don't slip back into your old ways of doing evil....now you must be holy in everything you do...You must be holy because I am holy." 1Peter 1:13-16 NLT

"...trust in God...your faith and hope can be placed confidently in God...have sincere love for each other as brothers and sisters... love each other intensely with all your hearts." 1Peter 1: 21-22 NLT

"...get rid of all malicious behavior and deceit... Be done with hypocrisy and jealousy and backstabbing. You must crave pure spiritual milk so that you can grow into the fullness of your salvation." 1Peter 2:1-2 NLT

"God is building you, as living stones, into his spiritual temple... you are God's holy priests, who offer the spiritual sacrifices..." 1Peter 2:5 NLT

"...for you are a chosen people. You are a kingdom of priests, God's holy nation, his very own possession. This is so you can show others the goodness of God, for He called you out of the darkness into His wonderful light." 1Peter 2:9 NLT

There are many passages of Scripture that I could have chosen to describe Grandma's life and its influence on mine. But, these are the ones that God led me to include in this section of the book. We all have special relatives or friends who have guided us and made significant changes in our lives.

Compassion for Others

One of the reasons I have included this story is for you to think about your role in the life of young people or children that you may be acquainted with. Your opportunities to share with them will pass by quickly, so it is important to act promptly. Children are always in need of compassion and being comforted. They do not know how to recognize and then verbalize their needs for such care. But, the need is there!

There are also needs with children that you do not know personally … in the schools, in day care centers, hospitals, through the Court systems, and other venues. My heart breaks as I think of children that I know, who are in great need of comforting, but are unable to receive it. Perhaps you are in the same situation.

I would encourage you to be observant and on the look-out for opportunities to serve children and young people with the gift of God's comforting grace. You don't have to be a grandparent to pass this gift on. You just need to be one of God's children desiring to be filled with His holiness ready to listen and pour out God's love into that person's life.

Golden Anniversary portrait of Grandma and Gramps Conklin June 1965 Hollywood, FL

Grandma and Gramps in their Poland living room with
Lois and Bette with their new baby dolls. Gifted with a
dry sense of humor, Gramps is peering over Lois.

Grandma and Gramps with Lois and Bette and their proverbial
Christmas card display. Poland house in early 1950's.

Front of the house we shared with Grandma and Gramps in Poland,
OH 1947-54. They lived on the left side; we lived on the right.

Side of the house in Poland. Lois and I shared
a bedroom on the second floor.

Barn on lower side of property in Poland. Our cars were parked in the barn. The raspberry patch was located next to the barn and the garden was close to the barn.

Memorial Methodist Church   *Poland, Ohio*

Memorial Methodist Church, Poland, Ohio, which was within walking distance of the house. The church burned to the ground not long after we moved to NC in 1956. It was built in beautiful classical style with stone, stained glass windows, a lovely working organ, and a classic church bell.

CHAPTER 8

Children Learn What They Live

Over the years, as I prepared to write the original book, I started gathering interesting pieces of writings and other notices that drew my attention. I placed them in various file folders and pulled them out to incorporate into the books when or where I felt they were worthy to be used. Following is a poem (author unknown) that fell into that category and I thought it was appropriate to include after writing about my Grandma and Gramps Conklin. There is no author or title that fits with this poem. I consider the words worthy to be included in the book about "Rising above our Life Journey."

If a child lives with criticism,
He learns to condemn,
If a child lives with hostility, He learns to fight.
If a child lives with ridicule,

He learns to be shy.
If a child lives with shame,' he learns to feel guilty.
If a child lives with tolerance, he learns to be patient.
If a child lives with encouragement, He learns with confidence.
If a child lives with fairness, He learns
justice. If a child lives with security,
He learns to have faith
If a child lives with approval,
He learns to like himself.
If a child lives with acceptance and friendship,
He learns to find love in the world.

Author Unknown

The LORD has told you what is good, and this is what He requires of you; to do what is right, to love mercy, and to walk humbly with your God. Fear the LORD if you are wise! Micah 6:8-9 NLT. In this passage, the Lord admonishes us about goodness, mercy, humbleness, and walking with God.

Front view of Poland Union Elementary School, that I attended Grades 1-5 (1950-1955). The school is still in use today. During a fire drill in first grade, I panicked and my teacher Mrs. Sitler had to hold me under her arm like a sack of potatoes and carry me out of the building.

Side view of Poland Union , where I attended fifth grade on the second floor. A tornado split at the school, sparing the lives of many children, as it went in two directions. Recently, a former class mate Bill Dornan verified this story when we met to visit.

CHAPTER 9

An Early Death

My father had been an active person with his gardening; keeping up his yard; and exterior of our house, in addition to his employment in the US space program. He also worked with the Boy Scouts at our church, enjoying the many range of scouting activities that he had participated in when he was a teenager, including being an Eagle Scout.

When he was growing up he **had been very sick and his parents had not been able to secure proper medical care for him because of their limited funds. It was during the time of the Depression, 1930's** and it was difficult to just put meals on the table. Unbeknownst to them, Cloud had been sick with rheumatic fever, which damaged his heart. During the interim years, he had participated in high school **cross country, track sporting events. He qualified to participate at the Ohio state level of**

competition, which included traveling to Columbus for the events. He placed to compete at first and second level positions for the events at the state level, representing his high school Poland Seminary, which was located in Poland, Ohio. It is amazing that he was able to achieve such success with the damage that was done to his heart by the rheumatic disease. As an aside, if I had not moved away from Poland, Poland Seminary would have been my Alma Mater.

In his forties, the disease began to affect his overall health. Appointments, while in his fifties, with specialists in the cardiac field, revealed damage to his heart that needed attention. He needed open heart surgery done soon, and the sooner the better. My sister Lois was seriously ill at the time with Lupus and Mom needed to go be with her. Mom was torn with the decision of what to do.

She finally opted to return to be with Daddy. I took a leave from my job and went to Florida to help her and Daddy. They had a thirty-one foot travel trailer which they drove to Lakeland, Florida, near western Florida from their home on the east coast of Florida to reside in and use as their base of operations. Daddy was scheduled for **surgery at Lakeland General Hospital.** It had a reputation of having the most up to date equipment and medical staff available at the time. We felt good about that.

I will never forget **our last hours together**. The night before his surgery, we did our patriotic duty by casting our absentee ballots. They cast their Florida ballots and I did my Georgia ballot. Daddy was a great believer in exercising our political rights. Then he spoke privately with me about the fact that he might not survive the surgery and **what he wanted me to do about my mom**. He was very specific, but made a lot of sense. It was carefully thought out.

Next he had Mom, himself, and me recite the 23rd Psalm together. He was really getting down to the nitty-gritty of everything. I knew that his father had studied all of the Psalms prior to his death and my own daddy was doing the same thing.

The next day was his **surgery and things did not go well**. His heart stopped during the procedure, but they **did revive him**. The piece of equipment that they needed to keep him alive was expensive and there was only one available in the state of Florida. They were able to get it to Lakeland in time to save Daddy's life. WOW!!!

The next time I saw Daddy he **looked like he had aged twenty years.** I had heard of such, but this was my first time to experience such an event. What a shock! His hair changed to the color grey. Mom and I decided to stay at a local motel rather than travel back and forth to the campground. We contacted my sister Lois who was still very ill with lupus at the time. She and her husband Fred decided to fly to Lakeland. My husband's employer flew him to Lakeland to be with us. Daddy's sister Ruth flew in from Denver, as well as her daughter Libby from Michigan. We all rallied around Daddy to encourage him to survive.

Why did I go into all this detail in this story? This was **my first true spiritual experience that I remember** that has had a lasting impression upon me. **Daddy never left the hospital. He died about six weeks later at the young age of 55.** It broke my heart, because I was a "daddy's girl." My own children would never have the opportunity to know their Boppa (grandfather). That fact caused me much grief and sadness.

My mom lived alone as his widow for the next forty years. Part of what was significant was the waiting room area. We befriended others who had family members who were also in **the ICU (intensive care unit.) We witnessed and prayed with them.** I had brought with me my copy of **J. B. Philip's New Testament translation of the Bible**. It was while I was reading it that I found **Romans 8:28** and the surrounding verses. Since then, that passage is very special to me.

"And we know that God causes everything to work together for the good of those who know God and are called according to His purpose for them." NRSV and JB PHILIP'S

CHAPTER 10

What Do You Mean? A Wild Horse

We had been busy building a new house in Fayetteville, GA, overseeing the construction ourselves. Most evenings and on Saturdays, we traveled the ten miles each way after work to see what work had been completed and what was on schedule for the upcoming days. We were excited about this new location that we would call our home.

<u>Aunt Clio and Aunt Ruth</u>

Jim's Aunt Clio, who was our spiritual mentor, had been instrumental in helping us decide on the particular lot in the chosen subdivision for our new home. She had **counseled us about our earthly home vs. our heavenly home, helping to keep us properly focused** on our intended investment. She wanted to be

91

sure that we were not becoming materialistic about this new home, to the point of ignoring our commitments to the Lord. We had never been personally challenged about our personal finances in such a manner before. But, it was a necessary part of our journey. There was no one better to be under the guidance of than Aunt Clio, for this lesson.

Aunt Clio, and her sister Aunt Ruth, were a very important part of our lives. Aunt Ruth took care of our children, Janet and Ricky, during the day while I worked. She sewed clothes for them, played with them, and taught them all about cooking. When Aunt Clio came home from work in the afternoons, she took the children for walks and taught them about God and Jesus. Unmarried, **Aunt Clio treated the children and Jim and I as hers, and called us her family.** Verses of Scripture flowed freely from Aunt Clio's tongue, during the course of any conversation with her.

It was significant that Aunt Clio was involved with the construction of our new home from the beginning, because of the challenges that we were to face. Of course, we had no way of knowing what the future held. She was the **steady rock for us.**

Remember the Bible verse about **building a house on solid rock?** All other ground is sinking sand. Do you remember singing the song?

In Matthew 6:19–21, 24 NKJV, Jesus teaches the following about our **material possessions:**

"Do not lay up for yourselves treasures on earth, where moth and rust destroy and where thieves break in and steal; but lay up for yourselves treasures in heaven, where neither moth nor rust destroys and where thieves do not break in and steal. For where your treasure is, there your heart will be also."

"No one can serve two masters; for either he will hate the one and love the other, or else he will be loyal to the one and despise the other. You cannot serve God and mammon."

"Mammon" refers to money, property, or wealth, gathering it for present or immediate enjoyment rather than investing in our future with Jesus.

Construction

Shortly after the initial work was done on the house, lumber building supplies and related items had been delivered for framing to commence. The next morning the general contractor Joe called to tell us that most of the supplies had been stolen during the night. We were shocked that such a thing could have happened.

Construction continued and we felt good about the progress. Then we received another call from Joe telling us that more lumber supplies had been stolen. All of the interior doors for the house were gone, and miscellaneous supplies were missing. Additionally, they had destroyed three exterior doors to the house during the break-in. **Once again we had to file an insurance claim.**

Another Break-In

One day in September, I came home from work, sensing that something was wrong as I drove into the garage. Then I realized that the door going into the house was demolished. Our sheltie dog wasn't at the door to greet me. The adding machine and typewriter were missing....the tools that I used to make my living. In the living room, Jim's ham radio equipment had been torn out of the furniture cabinet where it was kept. **When I went into our bedroom I felt like I had been violated, as I observed the mess.** Our bathroom was worse. I finally found our Sheltie outdoors. But, she never trusted men after that. Apparently, she had been mistreated and drugged.

I tried my best to protect Janet and Ricky from the horrors of what had transpired in our home. **What had once been a safe haven for them was now a source of fear**. When Jim arrived home, I collapsed into his arms. We thought that surely this would be the end of our misfortune.

Yet Another Break-In

Jim was determined that he was going to protect our new property. So, against my wishes, he moved a mattress down to the house and put it in one of the four bedrooms. At that time, cell phones were unheard of! He did not have a gun. Just Jim! And he was going to spend the night alone at the new house. At that time, Fayette County was very rural. There were only a few sheriff deputies and at night there were even fewer deputies on patrol.

Jim settled down for the night on the mattress and then he heard the sound of gunshots outside his window. And there was more than one of them and only one of him. Well, he had to **face the reality that his life might be at stake.** So, quickly, he exited the bedroom, ran down the stairs and left the house through the basement door, ran through the woods to the neighbor's house and aroused them from their sleep. Jim knew that they (the bad guys) would not see him leaving. Where we were building, there was only one house that was completed on our street. There were no houses on the street behind ours or on the streets on either end of ours. The lots were two acres in size and heavily wooded. At night it was very, very dark. In other words, it was secluded and Jim felt relatively safe.

The sheriff's deputy came so that Jim could file a report. The amazing thing is that the **deputy left one of his rifles with Jim for the rest of the night**, saying that he would pick it up in the morning. Somehow that had to be some type of "guardian intervention" from the "Heavenly realms." At that time, we did not personally know any of the county officials.

Break-Ins vs. the Insurance Company

Time was marching on and we had deadlines to meet. Then we received another call from Joe. Most of the copper tubing for the plumbing had been cut out in the basement. At this time copper yielded a healthy price in the salvage market. One of the furnaces was removed except for some jagged pieces of metal. This time when the insurance claim was filed, we were given notice that **the policy would be terminated in a few weeks**. Talk about stress! We were tired and wondered how we would get everything done before the insurance coverage would be cancelled.

Front view of Fayetteville house, under construction, showing all the trees in the yard. Camellia bushes are from plants started by Jim's father in the Fall of 1980.

**Back view of Fayetteville house, under construction, showing
all the trees and plants attached to the property in Fall 1980.**

<u>A Horse on the Loose</u>

One night in October, we were driving back home after checking
out the day's work. We were tired and the children were hungry. As
we were driving up West Bridge Road, Jim slowed down to about
15 mph to allow Janet and Ricky to see a white cat sitting on a fence.
Normally, he would have been driving about 45 mph in that section
of the road.

Since seat belts were not required, Ricky, who was three years
old, was standing on the front seat between Jim and me. Janet, who
was five, was sitting in my lap, in the front seat. Jim was driving our
1970 Chevrolet Impala, a heavy-duty regular sized passenger car. As
we rounded the curve in the road, a **huge horse was being chased
down the road towards us,** in our lane, by several kids and before
we knew it, the horse came up over the hood of the car, **shattering**

the windshield and tearing the roof backwards. There was the sound of broken glass and crunching metal. I heard a blood-curdling scream from my husband and then... **dead silence**. I knew that Jim was dead. There was no doubt in my mind.

I just sat there. I didn't move. Then I heard Jim say, "**Where are the kids?**"

I said to him, "what kids?" I was in such shock that I did not remember that we had children. "What kind of mother was I?" Then I felt Janet in my lap; my arms were still around her waist, as they had been before the crash.

But, where was Ricky? Had he been thrown out the open windshield? Or, the side window? I couldn't find him! Then I started to panic. Where was my precious son, Ricky? Later we found him on the floorboard, at my feet. He had miraculously fallen to the floor when the horse hit the car.

The **horse had boomeranged back off the car** and landed in front of it, on the roadway. Jim was bleeding from his head. Ricky wouldn't say a word. Others called for the police and an ambulance. All four of us were placed into one ambulance and taken twenty some miles to the hospital. Getting us put into the ambulance seemed to take forever. By the time we left the scene of the accident, nightfall was coming on and we could barely see anything.

Jim was placed in a hospital emergency room by himself and the children and I were placed in another room. I had no idea what was happening with Jim or what his condition was, since they kept me in a room with the kids. **No one could get Ricky to talk or respond, so we couldn't tell if he was hurt. That was really scary.**

CHAPTER 11

A Prayer of Thanksgiving

Later, the door opened and our pastor Rev. Bob Partridge walked in. Besides being our pastor, Jim and Bob were friends and they often attended sporting events together. We were very fond of Bob and I was extremely glad to see him, especially at a time like this. His attempts at getting Ricky to talk were also unsuccessful.

I will never forget the next thing that happened. In his gentle ways, Bob said to me, **"Let's have a prayer of Thanksgiving."** I thought Bob had lost his mind. What was he thinking? A prayer of Thanksgiving??? We had just had a major accident. Our car was totaled. Jim was injured and I didn't know how badly. **Ricky wouldn't respond and Janet just sat and looked**. And I was trying to hold everything together. And Bob wants me to thank God for this?

It was **time for me to understand about thanking God in a new and different way**. It is normal for us to pray and ask God for things. We do it all the time – give me a raise, take away this speeding ticket, make my baby well, let me pass this test. Afterwards, we may or may not thank God. We just kind of assume He will take care of things for us.

Bob was right. We needed to thank God that we were all alive and that our injuries were not life-threatening. The horse had hit Jim in the head. The police and insurance people told us that the way the roof of the car had been torn back, there was no way Jim should have lived.

He **should have been decapitated**. Instead, he only needed twenty-six stitches above his eyes. It was a miracle that he survived. Angels must have intervened when I heard Jim's screams. Now I knew what a prayer of Thanksgiving was and I would never forget.

"always thanking the Father." Colossians 1:12 ESV

Some friends of ours from church came to the hospital and later they drove us home. A few miles down the road from the hospital Ricky finally spoke, asking, **"did the horse live?"** We had to tell him, "No, the horse died in the accident."

Giving Thanks with a Grateful Heart

Through this entire journey we were also thankful that Aunt Clio was there by our sides praying for us and with us. She helped us stay focused and she kept us encouraged as we encountered the many **challenges that we had never expected as we were building the house**.

We learned many valuable lessons from her about being mentored in a Christ-like manner. That is important, because one day we would have our turn at mentoring others. In the future, we have had the opportunities to share about offering Prayers of Thanksgiving.

Following are part of the words from the song "Give thanks with a grateful heart". A passage of Scripture from Romans 5:3-5 NIV summarizes our journey of building our new house; the break-ins at both the new house and our old house; and the horse accident.

"but we also rejoice in our **sufferings**, because we know that suffering produces **perseverance**, perseverance **character**, and character, **hope**. And hope does not disappoint us, because God has poured out His **love** into our hearts by your hearts by the Holy Spirit, whom He has given us." Rom. 5:3-5 NIV

When we were utterly helpless, Christ came at just the right time and by sending Christ died for us sinners. Now, no one is likely to die for a good person, though someone might be willing to die for a person who is especially good. But God showed his great love for us by sending Christ to die for us while we were still sinners............................Yes, Adam's one sin brought condemnation upon everyone, but Christ one act of righteousness makes all people right in God's sight and gives them life." Rom.5:6-10 NLT.

One of my favorite praise songs is a suitable way to complete this story of God's compassion and grace as we learned many lessons through adversity. Often when I hear the words to the song or the music to it, I think of Bob Partridge and his visit to the hospital along with his teaching us about Prayers of Thanksgiving.

GIVE THANKS

Give thanks with a grateful heart
Give thanks to the Holy One
Give thanks because He's given
Jesus Christ His Son
And now let the weak
Say I am strong
Let the poor say I am rich
Because of what the
Lord has done for us.

CHAPTER 12

Testing Our Values

What do you do when your **value systems are tested to the nth degree?** Do you follow them or back down on what you have stood up for over the years? **Abortion is one of those subjects**. Jim and I did not believe in abortion of unborn babies. I had even participated in anti-abortion groups that met monthly and kept up with the Marches that happened locally and on a national level in January.

When I was thirty-seven, I found myself sick and unable to get better from a stomach ailment. None of the medications helped. Finally my family doctor suggested we test to see if I was pregnant. I insisted that wasn't possible because I had been so sick that the activity for becoming pregnant had not happened.

A few days later, his office called to tell us that **I was indeed PREGNANT**. We were shocked and distraught. Immediately I thought of all the twenty-some medications I had taken over the past several weeks and the X-rays and their possible **impact on the baby**. **Fear settled in** for the baby's health and well-being. The family doctor referred me to an OB/GYN that specialized in high-risk pregnancies. I made an appointment with him immediately.

We also contacted our church pastor with our concerns. At this time abortion was a "hot" subject. The doctor advised us that he had consulted with specialists at Emory University and the baby should be ok even though she had not had the protective uterine sac around her at the appropriate time during the pregnancy.

Much to our shock, **our pastor called us one afternoon and said that he had no problem if we decided to end the pregnancy.** Needless to say, we never returned to that church. Instead, we contacted Rev. Bob Partridge, who is mentioned in several other stories (horse accident story) and sought his counsel. He was very compassionate and understood our situation and encouraged us to go forth with the pregnancy, trusting God.

At the time, Jim was part of a men's study group that met weekly. When they came to our house, they **laid hands on my belly** and prayed for the baby. Nightly, Jim and I did likewise, before going to bed. Our friends rallied around us and we were living examples to them of carrying out our convictions.

We decided we needed to **tell Janet and Ricky** what was going on with Mama and the potential baby in case I had a miscarriage or the baby was born with birth defects. We explained the situation to them. Later, I found the following in Janet's Bible, **"God, please take care of our baby."** Such spiritual maturity for a ten year old.

I carefully followed the doctor's instructions the rest of the pregnancy. She arrived April 2, 1980, appearing healthy. In later years, we discovered that Cynthia Joy had some **birth defects**, but we have loved her just the same and dealt with those defects as they have reared their ugly heads. In the early years of school, we discovered she had **certain learning disabilities** that affected her reading and comprehension, that left her several grade levels behind.

As a young teenager, more birth defects started to emerge and we started on our merry-go-round of medical care. First to emerge were signs of **anaphylactic shock** events, during which we would have to call the EMT's to the house, as Cynthia lost consciousness and had trouble breathing. By the time we would get to the hospitals, no one could figure out the cause of the episodes. They were very scary! Over time, we got where we knew most of the county EMT's.

Next to come was a **dermoid ovarian cyst,** which brought Cynthia to the floor, doubled over in pain. It wasn't until a plain, old regular X-ray was taken that the abnormal and bizarre cyst was identified. I had never heard of such a phenomena before. It was necessary that surgery be performed to remove the abnormal cyst immediately.

At the age of 13, she began having episodes that involved irregular beats of her heart. The diagnosis was **(SVT) supra ventricular tachycardia**. She was put on medication by a pediatric cardiologist from the well-known and respected Emory University's Eggleston Children's Hospital. One day she had severe SVT and she was transported to Southern Regional Hospital in Riverdale. She was stabilized and we were discharged.

We went to the car and she went back into another episode of SVT. The doctors kept telling us they needed to see an episode in action. I hurried her back into the emergency department. The doctor expressed there was nothing they could do to save her life. I will never forget the look of fear and "what can I do" look on the doctor's face. All I could do was pray. Suddenly they were transporting her to Emory. I was panicking. Dr. Eddie Hulse, one of the pioneers in this type of children's surgery was out of the area training other doctors in the procedure Cynthia needed. Cynthia was put into a six- day holding pattern at Emory. Eventually her surgery day arrived and she survived. Glory to God!!! She had **experimental heart ablation surgery** with Dr. Hulse doing the procedure.

She had minor episodes of SVT during her pregnancies and currently she is having minor episodes. There is the possibility she may have to have it redone in the near future, as happens with others from time to time.

While recovering from the surgery, Cynthia was **sexually assaulted and raped. This led to emotional problems and she had to be hospitalized in a psychiatric hospital for several months**. It was a difficult time for all of us. None of these events would have changed our opinions about abortion and keeping our baby with potential birth defects. She has been a blessing to us in countless ways and taught us many lessons about life and God's gift of life.

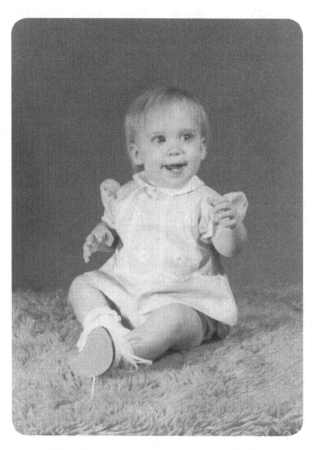

Baby Cynthia looking a good bit like her ten year older sister Janet.

CHAPTER 13

Facing My Fears

"Have I not commanded you? Be strong and of good courage; do not be afraid, nor be dismayed, for the LORD your God is with you wherever you go."

Joshua 1:9 NKJV

When you hear or read the word **"FEAR"** does it create within you any strong emotions or feelings that cause you to react from the neutral position that you were in immediately before the "fear" incident? Personally, I do react. **Often, it is with anxiety**. A switch is flicked. In the past, a photo of a snake would send me into a tizzy. I would promptly turn the page of the book. As a child, I would be plagued with nightmares. They would awaken me and bother me during the day. As I became older, those fears lessened and I became more in control of my world. In reading for this part of the writing of the book, I discovered that the word **"fear" is associated with "awe" or respect toward someone or something**. Previously, I was not aware of that. It is used in reference to admiration or respect to something that God has done.

There are countless verses or incidences of events with people experiencing fear because of God's actions. For example, the **shepherds were afraid when the angels approached them** announcing the birth of baby Jesus. In the stories of Moses and the Exodus from Egypt, there are many times of fear with the plagues of locusts and other creatures. **Growth of my faith has made a difference in how I handle fear and how I define it.** The personal injuries and health problems I have experienced have made fear something different.

I will be discussing that in more detail in my second book "Ugly Bears" when I present my life with injuries from an auto accident and auto-immune diseases. Overcoming fear was a constant as I had to **learn to walk again,** numerous times over the years with each surgery or onslaught of the illnesses. **Perhaps you have conquered little fears or have had to exercise courage to overcome huge fears in your life journey.**

Many times, in the book, I will refer to the fact that I was afraid about certain types of situations. In some ways I was more fearful than others my age, and in other ways I was less fearful than others. I **attribute some of my fears to the following situations in my life:**

> **Upbringing** – my mother and her mother, my Grandma Haley were skeptical about many things and expressed their fears openly, rather than hiding them from Lois and me. My mom was a perfectionist in her actions and expected the same from my sister Lois and me. This instilled certain fears in our actions. Writing this book has caused me to become even more aware of this behavior and my resulting reactions.

Living environment-most of the time I lived in relatively safe neighborhoods, but I was aware of unsafe locations where others lived.

College environment-the location of Case Western Reserve University (CWRU) was a culture shock for me. Poor, black neighborhoods surrounded the campus, as did certain ethnic groups of lower class, blue collar workers' homes, such as steel workers, construction workers, etc. The Cleveland Metro Rapid Transit system, that provided transportation for many ethnic riders, passed through the campus. Getting on the Rapid Transit from a CWRU campus station and then riding with those individuals, forced me to face my fears with those groups of people.

Working environment – after Jim and I married, when I first started working in central downtown Atlanta, I had to park our car in unsafe areas (such as enclosed, brick parking lot buildings) and then walk past homeless people, panhandlers, and others I felt unsafe around. For me, this was a challenge.

Accidents – several vehicle accidents or near accidents caused me to be fearfully cautious about the possibility of a repeat, in the future.

Natural disasters – past tornado and/or hurricane activity, and/or snowstorms made me fearful of future repeats. Having to evacuate our home or hotels while on vacation or drive away from a hurricane had been scary situations in the past.

Political or governmental incidents – the Civil Rights movement was the source of many unsafe events, as were other governmental related sorting outs of society.

Now that I look back on these events, some of my fears seem petty, while others still seem significant. **Fear may certainly have a bearing on how we experience our ongoing journey of life and how we rise above it.**

As I stated above, probably my longest living fear is that of **snakes**. When we lived in the big double house in Ohio, we often saw snakes in the garden areas. Daddy and Gramps were called upon to kill them. I will never forget the day I was walking to Scouting at the Presbyterian Church and a small garter snake was slithering in the grass beside the sidewalk. I totally lost it, screeeeeeamed, and acted like it was the end of the world. I was probably about seven years old at the time.

At the age of twelve, we lived in Matthews, NC, a sleepy suburb of Charlotte. Down the dirt road from where we lived, was a huge blackberry bush patch. My sister Lois and I had taken buckets with us to gather the succulent berries. We each had filled our pails nicely, when one of us spied a snake on the ground. As we ran out of the patch, we lost many of the berries out of our buckets. **So much for having Mom bake a blackberry pie!**

My other vivid snake memory is when we lived in Melbourne Beach, Florida. I was in the garage ready to enter the house, when I saw a snake at my feet on the steps entering the house. I quickly backed away and entered the house another way, getting my Mom. She killed the poisonous snake with a hoe.

Most of my other fear stories involve vehicles. In the late 1950's, Mom was driving the car through central Florida along the roads next to the canals through the Everglades. Dangerous roadways and unsafe drivers. Lois and I were in the back seat playing with our toys, oblivious to our surroundings and circumstances. All of a sudden we felt the car swerving and daddy yelling. He had just grabbed the steering wheel to keep us out of the canal. **Mom had lost control** of the car and we were headed for certain drowning in the Everglades.

Another vehicle incident happened at about age eight. Daddy had gone to college at Youngstown College and had a friend that lived in Sharon, Pennsylvania. One wintery night we drove from Poland to Sharon on icy and snowy covered roads. Sharon was a small town built on hills. As we proceeded up one hill, the car started slipping and sliding, with daddy unable to control its backward direction. I will never forget the feelings of fear from that incident and to this day, **I do not like riding on ice covered streets.**

I attended college in Cleveland, Ohio during the beginning of the Civil Rights movement in the 1960's. The atmosphere was the perfect set-up for another one of my times of great fear. Case Western Reserve University (**CWRU) was set in the midst of a poor African-American neighborhood, filled with gang activity and other unsafe activities.** One night in the 1960's, while on a date, my date and I had just walked past the practice fields for the Cleveland Browns football team. We started walking down one of the streets where numerous fraternity houses were located. All of a <u>sudden</u> **several young black punks started throwing rocks at us and yelling obscenities at the young man I was with and myself. We tried to ignore them and picked up our walking pace towards the fraternity house and safety.** I was forever scared and that incident was the source of fear for me in other situations in the future.

About the same time, my great **Aunt Blod died** in Youngstown, Ohio, which was about seventy-five miles away from the college campus. I decided to **ride the Greyhound bus** from their station which was just off the edge of the CWRU campus to Youngstown, with someone from the family picking me up there. I had purchased my ticket and was standing outside in the rainy weather in the midst of the Civil Rights atmosphere. **All of a sudden I was threatened with a black on white incident, as a young black attempted to steal my luggage.** I was already upset about my beloved Aunt Blod, but I was the young and naïve college student from the Deep South.

Somewhat related were the times when I had to **walk to and from the parking garages in downtown Atlanta after my night classes at Georgia State University. I was always somewhat afraid and on guard, as I walked through certain sections of downtown Atlanta and the areas approaching Grady Hospital.** Walking past the homeless and drunkards was not easy to do after 9:30 at night or on the weekends.

In the 1960's rioting broke out in Los Angeles after the Rodney King trial. In return, rioting broke out in other parts of the United States, including Atlanta. That day I was in downtown Atlanta for a huge continuing education conference at the CNN center for certified public accountants (CPA's.) **I had parked my car in an enclosed garage several blocks away, where I felt it would be safe** to get to my car late in the afternoon. News of the beginning of the California riots trickled into the coliseum. Shortly afterwards, we were updated that **rioting had begun in the nearby area**, but that changed. Cars were being overturned. Fires were started. Sirens were blaring. **Tension filled the conference center.**

The conference was stopped immediately. Leaders of the Georgia Society of CPA's announced that hotel rooms at the adjacent Omni hotel would be provided to members who felt it would be unsafe to get to their vehicles. Since my car was several blocks away, I decided to spend the night at the hotel. It **did not take an act of faith to spend the night with a lady I did not know nor had I seen before that day**. All night long, I heard the sounds of sirens and emergency vehicles and looking out the hotel windows I could see the fires.

When we lived in Melbourne Beach, Florida, and I was in my junior year of high school an incident happened that I wrote about later in a college Freshman English class assignment. The professor did not believe the story happened and gave me an F as my grade for my paper. **He just didn't understand how indoor heating worked in central Florida.**

We lived in an "L" shaped house with my parents' bedroom at one end of the "L" and my sister Lois' and my bedroom at the other end of the "L". For heat, we used little electric space heaters, one in each room. In our bedroom, Lois and I each had a twin bed**. It was a record cold night**. We each had a wool blanket at the foot of out beds. The space heater was running, placed equally between our beds. In the middle of the night I remember **pulling my sheets up and spreading them over my face because I was having difficulty breathing. As time passed, breathing became more difficult.**

I went out into the hallway and turned on the light. I noticed smoke and that it was hard to see anything. I went into the bedroom and found the wool blanket on top of the heater. I had kicked the blanket off of my bed**. The blanket was smoldering and emitting smoke. Without thinking about safety, I picked it up and proceeded to my parent's bedroom at the other end of the house, knocked on their door and told them about the blanket being on fire.**

We had a swimming pool in the back yard. Daddy came out of their room, grabbed the blanket and promptly threw it into the pool. I did not think and **left my sister in the bedroom with the smoke and potential fire.** It was the middle of the night!

Perhaps you can relate to some of these "fear" stories I have written about. I can tell you one thing. **My fear level has diminished over the years. How? By trusting the Lord**. When I am in a car now, I pray and ask for His protection. That brings about a different level of peace. How about you? Are you willing to pray and trust our Heavenly Father?

CHAPTER 14

The Revolving Playroom Ricky's and Cynthia's Friends and Grief

As a teenager, Ricky spent much of his time with his friends doing the music scene and art related activities. The bands he was part of, used to perform at some of the clubs in Atlanta. They also enjoyed outdoor activities, including camping, hiking, skate boarding, and white-water kayaking in the mountainous areas of north Georgia, South Carolina, North Carolina, and Tennessee. **The kayaking activity caused me a lot of anxiety because of the possibility of injury in the rivers filled with huge boulders and dangerous water holes**. I prayed for their safety, but should have trusted the Lord more each time they engaged in those activities.

Our house was the gathering place for many of their events and music practice sessions which were very noisy. **Our neighbors were**

not always happy with all of their noise. I remember them coming to the door, asking us for quiet. In time, many of the guys came to love Jim and me. Ricky asked us **several times if different ones could live with us, while his friend(s) were working through difficult times with their parents**. Even years later after they moved out, they referred to Jim and me as Dad and Mom when they would come by to visit. We like to think that we had an influence on their Christian life and other important values. There were a few things that happened during those years that we had no influence over and we felt badly that we couldn't help these young men with the issues at hand.

The day that I had the spinal fusion surgery done on my neck, after the auto accident with the drunk driver, Ricky's friend Scott Owens was **killed in the early morning when he lost control of his car and hit a tree.** I felt badly that I could not be there for Ricky and a few of his friends. Since I knew some of his girl and guy friends fairly well, they did come to the hospital to see me. I spoke with them about Scott, extending sympathy, as I was able, while coming out of the effects of the anesthesia and the effects of the pain medications. I always regret that time of not being completely available, even though I couldn't help it. Lee, Jason, and a few others remain friends with Ricky to this day. Today Richard has an influence on others with his Christian values and beliefs. It has been interesting to watch his witness on social media such as Face book, as he shares with them.

Cynthia lost one of her friends in an automobile accident one evening as Mandy lost control of her car. Mandy, who was also a high school senior, hit a tree. That was a sad time for Cynthia. I remember attending the somber calling hours and sad funeral service and burial with her. At her wedding to Casey, Cynthia honored Mandy with special music.

Both Ricky and Cynthia have had to face similar tragic situations of death at early ages. Both of them lost one of their close friends at an early age. Mandy died as a high school senior when

Cynthia was a high school junior. The situation was similar with Ricky's friend, Scott.

Jim and I have maintained an attitude of openness with Ricky and Cynthia's friends in providing social and spiritual support for them as individuals and children of God needing help and/or compassion in their lives. We have tried to be non-judgmental with these young people at their time of need. Sometimes it has worked out and unfortunately, at other times, it has been the source of other problems for us.

CHAPTER 15

The Persistent Tornado

Tornados are frequent weather events in our area of the country. One particular tornado stands out in my memory because of its potential to harm any one of our three children or ourselves. It was a rough evening.

This particular tornado started in west Georgia, fraught with damaging and deadly potential, **headed toward our area**. Our first concerns were that it was headed through Newnan towards Fayetteville. Our youngest daughter Cynthia and her two girls lived about twenty-five miles away, in Newnan and we lived in Fayetteville. We watched the weather reports, heard the tornado sirens, and were very concerned. We prayed. The power went off and on. The winds howled. The lightning and thunder continued.

Then as storms are prone to do, **the direction shifted slightly and now the tornado was headed toward Grantville where**

our oldest daughter Janet and her son Andrew lived. Then the sirens warned our area again. The cable TV went off, which meant we lost contact with our updates. My husband and I went to the basement. The storm intensified. I went back upstairs to see if the cable had returned.

As I looked toward the TV, there was a big, black, blank screen. Then it quickly flicked on and I caught enough of the announcer's information to know that the direction had changed once again. It was **headed down the roads close to our son Ricky and his family in Senoia. I couldn't believe it.** Then the TV went dark once again. God had allowed me to see just enough to know how I was to pray. My first instinct was to grab my cell phone and call Ricky. But, I knew that would not be the best thing to do, because **I needed to allow my son to do whatever he had to do to be safe.** Now that is hard for a mother to do. I started praying for the Lord to spare their lives and to protect them. Essentially what I did was "**go to the throne of God and not to the phone of the world.**"

About five minutes later, I called Ricky. He and our granddaughter Jewel were in a closet. In a shaky voice that reflected shock, he told me that he had **heard the sound of a train. He had grabbed Jewel's hand;** they got into a closet, and started praying. Then he told me about **hearing objects hitting the sides of the house and the roof.** They lost electricity. Later he told me about using a flashlight to see that their yard was trashed. Eventually they were able to account for all of their horses and other animals. The horses were important because Jewel competed in pole and barrel horse racing events.

The next morning, they realized that parts of a house trailer were in their yard. Later they found out that those parts came from a trailer that was the **home of two people who were killed by the tornado.** Further inspection of the property enabled Ricky to determine the path that the tornado had taken. Downed trees, stripped bark and other evidence told the story. From the maps of the weather service and the damage, it was evident that the **tornado had**

been headed straight for their house. Miraculously, there was a definite turn to the path of the tornado, shortly before it reached their house. They were spared by about a hundred feet. When I saw the visual truth, I just broke down and cried. There was no doubt in my mind that prayers had saved Ricky and Jewel and their home. **Ricky's wife Jeri was at work throughout this ordeal**.

The same tornado which had threatened our youngest daughter, our oldest daughter, our son, and us had been diverted numerous times. Going to the throne of God had been our salvation. Is your relationship strong enough that you could trust God in similar circumstances? Personally, I have had one other close call with a tornado. In the fifth grade of elementary school, in Poland, Ohio, a tornado rushed into town, came down the main street and turned up the street that the old elementary school was located on. As it approached the one side of the old brick building, the tornado split into two sectors with one part going one direction and the other part going the opposite direction. **This prevented damage to the old school building and potentially loss of children's lives.**

I will never forget that day. I remember that our class was reciting the Lord's Prayer at the time the tornado split at the school building. That was in the days when prayer was allowed in schools. During a recent visit with a former classmate from that era, Bill Dornan verified the details of the above story.

"For I know the plans I have for you"

Jeremiah 29:11 NASB

"For I know the plans I have for you," declares the LORD, "plans for welfare and not for calamity to give you a future and a hope. Then you will call upon *Me* and come and pray to Me, and I will listen to you. You will seek *Me* and find Me when you search for Me with all your heart." Jeremiah 29:11-13 NASB

CHAPTER 16

Daddy Messed Up

The last words we expected to hear from our two and a half year old grandson Andrew James Kenney after we arrived at his home on August 21, 1999, were "Daddy messed up!", but that was what he had to say to Jim and me when we arrived on Jekyll Island, Georgia at his home and he woke up from his sleep.

After we arrived there, Jim had gotten into Andrew's bed with him for the rest of the night. Andrew spoke the words to his Grandpa Mabry when he realized who was with him. The words just broke our hearts further, as we had dealt with the events of the previous day. It was past midnight and we were tired and emotionally drained after learning that **Andrew's father Chris had committed suicide the night before.**

Our daughter Cynthia had been in the hospital after returning home from her honeymoon, having just been married three weeks

123

beforehand. We had just returned home early from our vacation to Florida. We were in the **beginning stages of shock, related to the various stages of grief. During May, we had lost three of our favorite relatives**, including Jim's Aunt Clio (our spiritual mentor), my Grandma Haley (a protector), and my father's sister, Aunt Ruth (one of my heroines).

We were emotionally exhausted, because they were all instrumental in our everyday lives in countless ways. We had been to Ohio for Grandma's funeral and disposal of her assets. Friends provided airline passes to Denver, Colorado for Aunt Ruth's funeral and disposition of her ashes at Mt. Evans, in the Rocky Mountains, This had allowed us to be with various cousins and other relatives to celebrate her life. A quick trip to north Georgia gave us the opportunity to be with Jim's family, at which time Jim officiated at the service for Aunt Clio. Grandma died at the age of 99 and since there would be few in attendance, my mom had Lois's husband Fred and my Jim officiate at her service. **This was probably the saddest time of my life…the loss of all these precious people in such a short period of time.**

Chris's suicide was a total shock to all of the family and friends, including his wife, who was our daughter Janet. It is never an easy event for anyone. Accordingly, this is the most difficult chapter to write for this book.

I have delayed writing it until the other chapters have been written. It is my desire to **write this with compassion and emotional sensitivity**, especially for Janet and Andrew and other surviving family members, whose hearts are still aching from his demise. We all still miss Chris and see him in Andrew's natural actions. He has grown up into a wonderful young man, whom we are all very proud of in his growth and chosen professional field of youth ministry.

As a single mom, Janet has done an outstanding job of raising Andrew, utilizing the support of family, church friends, Scouting, baseball teams, and other groups of people. Janet lived as a widow for fourteen years and in time, the **Lord provided her with a loving and**

caring husband, David Jacobs, whom, she married in June 2013. David has been a devoted, supportive, and Godly father to Andrew, for which we are all very grateful. David's parents/family have been a great addition to those supporting Andrew in his chosen journey. Presently, Andrew is pastoring at a mega church in the Pittsburgh, Pennsylvania area and plans to be married in February, 2020.

Recognizing that **suicide is a controversial subject**, and subject to a wide range of personal opinions regarding the actual act of suicide and its effects on other people's lives, my writing about this tragedy in our family is to raise **awareness of the need for compassion toward families that are faced with this situation and their need for support in continuing their family unity and protection of the innocent victims.** Usually there are other circumstances involved with the suicide and it is not our responsibility to judge others in what was happening within the family unit, but we are called to love them and support them as they attempt to continue their lives. **Andrew is an example of a young man who was well loved in a Christian home setting, with the goal of achieving good, rather than lashing out in anger against the legal system that let them down and led to the actions that triggered Chris' suicide.**

While in high school, Janet dated a few young men and enjoyed the dating scene as most normal teen girls did at that time in the 1980's. When she attended Emory University, as a freshman, she decided to join one of the sororities on campus and participate in that type of social life. She also worked part time on campus at Emory Hospital to earn spending money. While doing that she met an interesting young man, Chris Kenney, who was quite like her in many ways.

During the summer between her freshman and sophomore years, she worked on campus at a summer job, residing in an apartment near campus. My birthday was on August 4th and she decided to bring Chris to meet Jim and me that evening. To impress me, Chris brought me a single pink rose in a vase to say, "Happy Birthday." He was a catch from the beginning.

He was scheduled to graduate a year before her. They continued dating through her graduation from Emory in June 1992. They married in June 1992 in Fayetteville, Georgia, the town in which she grew up. After the wedding, Chris started studying for his Master's in Medical Science for a Physician Assistant degree at Emory and Janet began working on her Master's degree in counseling at Georgia State University.

Chris' mother's parents lived in a home on Jekyll Island, Georgia. Grandpa died shortly after Chris graduated with his Physician Assistant degree. Since his Grandmother (Ggma) needed someone to care for and live with her, Chris' mother asked Chris and Janet to sell their home in Lithonia (Atlanta) and move to Ggma's and assume responsibility for her and the remodeling of her house. Grandma was known as Ggma after Andrew was born. In 1996, Janet completed her Masters' degree; they sold their home in Lithonia and moved to Jekyll Island. Shortly after moving, Janet became pregnant with Andrew. Chris became involved with the remodeling project of the house, doing much of the work himself. Additionally, he sought employment in the medical field whereby he could utilize his degree from Emory.

Andrew was born May 13, 1997, in Savannah after Janet was hospitalized with pre-labor complications for several weeks. I went to South Georgia, during that time to help with Ggma's care and however else I could help with Janet's needs during that time. My time mentioned traveling back and forth between Savannah and Jekyll was a one hundred mile trip, each direction on the interstate, fighting truck traffic. It was very tiring. After Andrew was born, I stayed with them to help Janet, as any other new grandma would do. I noticed that Chris's behavior was not quite normal—a little off from the usual personality/social traits of our Chris.

Over Labor Day weekend, Jim and I, along with our son Ricky and daughter Cynthia went to Americus to be with Chris's parents at their home for a family gathering. Chris's father, Rev. Jim Kenney was the pastor at the Methodist church in town. After church, we had a southern style family dinner. Chris spent much time reading the Sunday newspaper, spread out on the floor, interested in the big story of the day....the death of Princess Diana in Paris. To me, **his actions were somewhat aloof that day.**

The next evening Janet called us to say that Chris had told her that **he was in trouble with the law and would be arrested the next day,** on Tuesday. He admitted to her that he had an **addiction problem** with Vicodin, a narcotic and had been abusing it and other pain medicines. He had taken eighty pills over the weekend. The scary thought to us was that he had been driving Janet and Andrew the lengthy distance between Americus and Jekyll, endangering their safety. That explained his aloofness over the weekend. Chris had surgery the previous fall, in October when Hurricane Opal hit Atlanta, and he had been given narcotics for pain relief during recovery. At that time, he became addicted to the pills. Working in a physicians' office, he had access to obtaining them much easier than most people. (Narcotics laws/control rules were much different in those days than they are today.)

Under the control of the legal system and their control of his case and convictions, Chris stayed clean of the use of all narcotics for two years, less two weeks. **He was following the mandates of the drug court in an orderly fashion, attempting to get his Physician Assistant's license re-instated,** to its previous status.

Prior to this time, there had not been an established drug court process in place in Glynn County (Brunswick), and the terms of his legal plan were being set in place in a "do as you go along" basis. His sentence included going to drug court five days a week, attending AA meetings several times a week, working full time, being a husband and a father. It was all set up in a developmental program, deciding how/what to do, as each day passed.

Chris was doing well with the program he was mandated to follow, even with all its pressure on his time and daily lifestyle and the fact that it was uncertain how it was going to be developed. Chris did not know how his program was going to be changed or upgraded from day to day or in the future. Chris was recognized for his leadership abilities and when drug court personnel were not available they would have Chris lead the discussions during the meeting times.

He was the only one in the program who had not had to drop out and restart at the beginning of the program. According to some of the participants, on two consecutive evenings, one of the counselors decided to pick on Chris and see if they could break him in front of the others.

Apparently, it worked. That second night, after drug court, Chris went back to his place of employment, a respiratory therapy firm, and updated the medical charts for each of his assigned patients. He ascertained that everything that needed to be done professionally for the company was accomplished before he laid his keys on his desk and left the building. **That was the Chris we knew and loved. Caring about his patients and their welfare.**

He exercised the same attitude for his employer. He was determined to beat his addiction and turn his life around for his son and wife. He wanted his professional license re-instated. He knew his family loved and supported him and were not there to judge him. I had gone to their home numerous times to stay and help them in whatever way I could during his recovery process.

It reminds me of the Bible story in which Jesus supports the woman who was being condemned by the men on the street and Jesus instructed them to throw a stone at her if they were without guilt. Often, we want to condemn others for their sins, when we are just as guilty or more so. The story from John 8:1-11 NLT is as follows: Jesus returned to the Mount of Olives, but early the next morning he was back again at the Temple. A crowd soon gathered, and he sat down and taught them. As he was speaking, the teachers of religious law and Pharisees brought a woman they had caught in the act of adultery. They put her in front of the crowd.

"Teacher," they said to Jesus, "this woman was caught in the very act of adultery. The law of Moses says to stone her. What do you say?

They were trying to trap him into saying something they could use against him, but Jesus stooped down and wrote in the dust with his finger. They kept demanding an answer, so he stood up again and said, "All right, stone her. But let **those who have never sinned throw the first stones! Then he stooped down again and wrote in the dust**.

When the accusers heard this, they slipped away one by one, beginning with the oldest, until only Jesus was left in the middle of the crowd with the woman. Then Jesus stood up again and said to her, "Where are your accusers?

Didn't even one of them condemn you? "No, Lord," she said. And Jesus said, "Neither do I. Go and sin no more."

The difficult part of Chris' actions has been the sadness and associated depression for Andrew, Janet, and Chris' parents, Jim and Janis Kenney (deceased), and his siblings, Celeste, Carole, and Cal. Of course, it has been difficult for us also. A short time after his death, Janet felt the call to enter the ministry and she applied **to attend seminary** at Candler School of Theology at Emory University. **She and Andrew moved in with Jim and me for the next three years, while she went to Emory**. Our life changed tremendously while they were with us. Grandpa and Andrew played a lot of baseball, which continued on into Andrew's teen years. Andrew attended the pre-school program at our church Hopewell United Methodist Church. My daily duties included getting him to and from pre-school.

Chris' suicide also affected Cynthia emotionally. She and Casey had only been married for three weeks when Chris died. One of those weeks, she had been in the hospital, sick and undergone several surgeries. We had to have her discharged early from the hospital to take her with us to Jekyll when we left to go be with Janet for Chris' funeral. Casey had a difficult time understanding how Chris could leave Andrew without a father and that created certain discord. For Jim and me, it was **sad watching both of our daughters suffer from these circumstances.** I involved myself in personal counseling and support groups. I found it difficult to find time to grieve for the other deaths in my family. For Jim and me, we had to work at learning **where to draw the lines**

or boundaries with Andrew and Janet, since we were the parents/grandparents and semi-parent/guardians.

Eventually, I established Grief Support groups at our church for dealing with the Thanksgiving, Christmas, and New Year's holiday season, sponsored by the Stephen Ministry program. These groups successfully served a wide variety of grieving citizens in the community for several years.

Andrew summed the situation up correctly and he has handled his life well considering the circumstances: "Daddy messed up." **Andrew has walked holding the hand of Jesus and accepted the love from his family. Compassion has been one of the keys to surviving the last twenty years.**

Chris was a well- loved person and well known, considering his age. He died at the young age of thirty years and Janet was twenty-nine years old. Attendance at the calling hours was overwhelming with others who were attendees at the drug court. They could not believe what had happened and we, the family were placed in the "uncomfortable" position of comforting them in their grief.

The funeral service was held at the Jones Auditorium at the Methodist Center on St. Simon's Island, Georgia (Epworth by the Sea) with standing room only. After the service, the closest family members gathered in the tiny chapel by the river and we had a quiet time of worship and prayer. Then we walked around the chapel and scattered some of Chris's ashes amidst the azalea bushes and other plants by the chapel building and on into the river area, which he had enjoyed over his lifetime of living in the area. St. Simons was a popular retreat area for youth of the South Georgia area.

Grandson Andrew Kenney, age 2 ½ years, living in great- Grandma Roberson's home on Jekyll Island, GA., Christmas after his daddy died.

Baptism of Andrew Kenney at UMC at St. Simon's Island with
Carol Lee, Chris Kenney, Janet Mabry Kenney, Rev, Jim Kenney,
Janis Kenney (d), Cal Kenney, and Mildred Roberson (d).

Baptism of Andrew Kenney at UMC at St. Simon's Island
with Jim Mabry, Chris Kenney, Janet Mabry Kenney, Bette
Conklin Mabry, and Lorraine Haley Conklin.(d)

CHAPTER 17

Tidbits About Lois's Lupus

My younger sister Lois was the first in the family to experience the ravages of auto-immune diseases. Lupus hit her at the age of twenty-five with a fifty-some day stay in the hospital. Doctors had a difficult time diagnosing the lupus and did not understand her condition. My mom went to Detroit to assist with her care.

I followed later, taking Janet, age five with me and Ricky, age two. In the middle of the winter, it was not an easy task with two young children. She had a mixed cocker spaniel dog named Taffy, who was a real challenge/handful for me. One afternoon, I had Janet and Ricky out in the snow playing. Not only did they get **messy with the snow**, but Taffy did a triple job of getting messy. I had to get dinner ready and clean her up enough to get her into the basement to give her a bath. With her long shaggy hair, water flew everywhere. The kids and I all got wet. Lois and her husband Fred laughed at me and the dilemma I was in. Today, it is a family joke. Fred went out and got fast food for supper. He also brought back the book "Cinderella" and another children's book.

Ricky fell asleep eating his meal. Fred read Cinderella, **naming the Prince the "Dude"** creating laughter for the kids. What a day. We were being **introduced to auto-immune life**. And I was helping my sister with compassion.

I will never forget after I returned home and being in church. All of a sudden I started praying fervently for Lois. I didn't know why, but the **prayers were intense**. When I got home, after a phone call, I knew why. A **blood clot was lodged in her left lung** and her life was in jeopardy. God was directing my prayers for my sister. What an experience! Over the years, I made several trips to assist with Lois's care, with the children in tow. By this time, Cynthia was part of our family and the drive to Detroit was more intense driving by myself. In the background, I was preparing for my own future experiences.

Lois's family visiting Janet's at Jekyll Island, GA home with
Rev. Uncle Fred Finzer, Aunt Lois Finzer, Janet Mabry
Kenney holding baby Andrew, and her son Brian Finzer.

CHAPTER 18

Coping with Unusual Events

Grandma Conklin always talked about life being a journey and us not being aware of what would be in store for each day of our travels. Below are thoughts about two experiences that have had profound effects on us and yet were completely unexpected. Just about everyone has personal feelings about these days. September 11 was a worldwide event. Each has spiritual significance and connection with the Lord, along with compassionate type connections. A murder is subject to affecting an unpredicted number of individuals.

Unfortunately, Cynthia has known two men who have been murdered. Each crime has been a terrible emotional strain on her, both at the time it happened and afterwards. Murder is one of the Ten Commandments discussed in the book of Exodus. It is an action that an individual is not to commit according to the instructions God gave to Moses for the people regarding their behavior.

The first murder was that of Robert Groeniger, the best friend and employer of her husband Casey. We were on vacation in the Tetons National Park in Wyoming when Cynthia called us to say that Robert had just been murdered by one of his business associates with numerous gunshot wounds.

My immediate reaction was to tell Cynthia that her life would never be the same. It would be forever changed, no matter what. Robert was a major influence in her life, both with her relationship with her husband and her financial situation. Robert had a great influence on Casey's actions and behavior. Life would be different for Cynthia's marriage and children.

We were in one of the rest areas of the Park when we were talking with Cynthia. It was fairly evident to others that something serious and emotionally draining was happening with us. Another couple started talking to us in comforting tones, asking if they could be of help. God was providing us with care two thousand miles away from home, in the middle of nowhere in forest land. They prayed for us and spent about a half hour of their vacation time with us. Praise God! Would you be willing to do that? What kind of attitude would you show? Loving or judgmental? When we returned home from our vacation, we returned to a completely different world.

"For God so loved the world that He gave His only Son that whoever believes in Him shall not perish, but have eternal life." John 3:16 NLT

Several years later, Jim and I went on a long, awaited trip to Utah, Arizona, and Montana to visit several of the National Parks that we had been planning to visit. We were very excited about the trip and the prospects of seeing the sites we wanted to see. We were in the southern part of Utah, having just seen the Coral Pink Sand Dunes National Park, one of the Utah State Parks. We had started early in the morning, allowing for the time zone adjustments.

As we were walking back to our car, we encountered another couple who were preparing to enter the trail. They greeted us by asking us a question: **Did we know about the World Trade Center being hit? And another hit?** Our first thoughts were of our nephew Gary Finzer who lived close to the Trade Center. Since we were in rural Utah, radio reception was poor.

September 11 was happening and we were in rural America. How scary! When we got to the North Rim of the Grand Canyon at the Visitor Center, there was no communication available. No television transmission. No radio news updates. There was a total hush to the area. No sound. **We had to call home to Atlanta and talk to our children on pay phones to find out what was happening.** When we got to Page, Arizona at the Colorado River, the roads were closed. The huge electric plant that served a wide area of customers was closed down with **security measures in place. Talk about an eerie feeling.** Pure EERIENESS!!! The rest of our trip was bizzare.

The remainder of our vacation was restless and unusual. It was so strange that any time we wanted any news update we had to call home to Atlanta. Our flight home was changed to a flight from Phoenix, Arizona on another date. Our site-seeing was changed because of road closures and security measures. **People were extra nice and considerate with each other. The** event 9-1-1 created an air of compassion, unlike anything else we had ever seen. Our seats on the airplane were changed to first class, with only a handful of us at that status. **It was an experience I never want to repeat again!**

> "Praise the Lord, all nations,
> Laud Him, all people!
> For His lovingkindness is great toward us,
> And the truth of the Lord is everlasting.
> Praise the Lord." Psalm 117:1-2NASB

I have included this Psalm because the 9-1-1 event included victims from countries all over the world and their families.

Psalm 116:1-5 NASB, addresses our individual spiritual needs, in situations of unusual needs. Our God is always present, no matter what.

"I love the Lord, because He hears
My voice and my supplications.
Because He has inclined His ears to me.
Because I shall call upon Him as long as I shall live.
The snake of death encompassed me
And the withers of Sheol came upon me.
I heard dizziness and sorrow
Then I called upon the name of the Lord
O Lord, I beseech You, Save my Life!"
Gracious is the Lord, and righteous.
Yes, our God is compassionate."

CHAPTER 19

An Iraqi Tragedy –
1LT Robert W. Collins–Our Hero

Robert Collins started attending Hopewell United Methodist Church in Tyrone, Georgia, when he was ten years old. **Both his parents were close to retirement as Lt Colonels from the Army when they moved to Tyrone with their only child Robert. We all became very fond of Robert,** as we watched him grow up into a fine young man. He was active in the youth programs at Hopewell; he played football and other sports at Sandy Creek High School across the street from the church; and participated in many other activities.

Our daughter Janet lived with us while she was attending seminary at Emory's Candler School of Theology. During part of that time, she taught the high school Sunday school class that Robert attended. Janet used to say that she saw some type of ministry career in the future for Robert. She said that because of his strong and abiding faith and willingness to be a disciple. Janet saw something extra-special in Robert and she never let go of those feelings!

West Point Military Academy

We were proud of Robert when he went to the United States West Point Military Academy at West Point, and we always looked forward to his visits to Hopewell. We were charmed by his friendly personality, jokes, and infectious smile. It didn't matter what our age was, he always had a kind word for everyone. **Robert's decision to attend West Point was his personal decision, based on the events of 9-11.** It was not based on promptings from his parents' careers, as so often happens in military families.

Robert's Family

After moving to Tyrone, Robert's mother **Sharon pursued a second career in education.** She completed additional degrees and worked in the local public and private school systems. It was obvious that Sharon had the gifts that were necessary to stimulate educational growth with children. And, she had the skills necessary for administrative responsibilities. Robert's father **Deacon pursued a second career of teaching specialized courses, traveling around the world for various corporations.**

Since Sharon was **one of the Stephen Ministers** at Hopewell and I was the leader of the program, we had the opportunity to become well acquainted with each other. We had time to share through the **training and service phases of Stephen Ministry.**

Off to IRAQ

After Robert **graduated from West Point in 2008**, we were all excited that he was coming back to Georgia for further training before being shipped out on a permanent assignment. Then we heard the word that he was being **assigned to Iraq**. We felt different feelings for Robert and his parents. It was all a different sense of reality. I remember asking Sharon specifically how she felt about the assignment. Also thinking how I would have felt if it were my son Ricky going to Iraq. Since both of Robert's parents were retired Lt Colonel's from the Army, they had way different feelings and experiences to draw upon than I did.

Robert left in October 2009 from Ft. Stewart, near Savannah, Georgia to assume his assignment near Mosul, Iraq. When he left, his parents and long-time girlfriend Nicolle Williams traveled with him, as far as they were allowed. I have seen photographs from those days, but I can't even begin to imagine what kind of feelings Sharon, Deacon, and Nicolle experienced during those hours.

Robert was adequately prepared for his assignment. He was well trained from one of the best military academies – West Point. Robert was physically fit. Granted he was short, but he was mighty and knew how to handle his body. He was well loved by his family, friends, church, fellow service members, and community. He knew how to be a friend to others and how to reach out in service and love to others. Above all, he loved the Lord. And, we all knew that.

There is a quote that some of us have seen and heard from Robert over the years. In some ways, it gives you an idea what kind of person Robert was,

"Life is a much easier beast to tame with
a little laughter and good will."

That quote always provides a chuckle for me. After writing this chapter, I gave Sharon a copy to review for correctness of dates and such. **Sharon commented "Never knew this."** What an interesting thing to learn about your child! I called our mutual friend Mike Nix and conveyed to him the details of the story. It brought a huge smile to his face. **A lesson in listening to God moments.**

We felt like **we were part of Robert's assignment in Iraq as we received photos by way of the Internet.** The soldiers in their desert uniforms. The tanks. The wooden office buildings. Elementary set ups of computers and supplies. Award ceremonies. Everyone making the best of the situation they were in! Names and faces were put together.

These soldiers were part of the **3rd Infantry Division of the United States Army.** Robert, who was twenty-four years old, was serving as a Platoon Leader to support Operation Iraqi Freedom.

An email like no other

After supper on April 8, 2010, I sat down at my computer to check my emails and glanced over the subject titles. One in particular stood out. It had Robert's name in it. I quickly opened it.

> **"1LT Robert Collins**, son of Deacon and Sharon Collins, **died in Iraq** on Wednesday, April 7, 2010, when the vehicle he was riding in hit an IED. He and his driver died, the other five members riding in the back of the vehicle survived."

My heart was broken, just as countless others were being broken as they received the same news.

Shock! No, it couldn't have happened to Robert.

What about Sharon. His dad? What must they be feeling? And his high school sweetheart?

My husband Jim wasn't home. I had to talk to someone, so I picked up the phone and started calling friends.

Our HERO

Our whole area went into mourning............. Everyone wanted to do something to help. .... As the different events unfolded over the next week, the roads were lined with people, young and old............ School children lined the streets. .... Offices let their employees out. .... Fire trucks raised their ladders.................... Flags were flying everywhere....................TV cameras and newspaper journalists were capturing the stories..............People hugged each other, all because we loved Robert and **our hearts were sad. Robert was our HERO**!

The Formal Tributes

During the days after learning of Robert's death, his parents and Nicolle traveled to Dover AFB for the dignified transfer of remains. Robert, his father Deacon, and the Rear Detachment Commander flew from Dover AFB to Peachtree City, Georgia. **Robert's remains travelled in the Parrott Funeral Home Model T hearse past his schools and church.**

Then there were the calling hours at the local funeral home. Saturday the funeral was held at the largest church in Fayette County, with both military and religious services. And, in keeping with Robert's personality, we shared some laughter as we viewed photos of precious family times. Hundreds and hundreds of motorcycles, emergency vehicles, police, and private vehicles participated in a **thirty-mile caravan to the cemetery to lay his body at rest.** I will never forget observing how the roadways were lined with people all along the route, as I drove my car in the procession. Everyone wanted to show their respect for this young man who had so unselfishly given his life, the ultimate sacrifice.

For most of us at the funeral and the burial, this was a first time and hopefully only time, to experience the death of an active service person. The experience has **given me a different sense of respect**

for the military, even though I grew up with military families while in high school. My sense of compassion for the military has taken on a different sense of perspective. Robert was the first member of his West Point class to perish.

A Father's Tribute

The **most striking display of emotion for me was Robert's father Deacon, as he gathered under the tent** at the cemetery, for the final portions of the services. Deacon was dressed in his full-dress uniform of the Army, honoring his son. It had probably been many years since he had **worn his dress uniform**. With his **face void of emotion, he stood erect at the proper times and places.** At other times, I observed slight movements of his hands.

What a difficult time for a father....losing his only child, his son, a fellow soldier. I felt all the compassion I could, but there was nothing I could do at that moment in time. My option was to pray for Deacon in his time of need.

The Opportunity for a Biblical Comparison

"For I am already being poured out as a drink offering, and the time of my departure is at hand. I have fought the good fight. I have finished the race. I have kept the faith. Finally, there is laid up for me the crown of righteousness, which the Lord, the righteous Judge, will give to me on that Day, and not to me only but also to all who have loved His appearing."

2Timothy 4:6–8 NKJV

At the time of Robert's death, his mother taught an adult Sunday school class, as did I. When I heard of his death, I searched my heart for something meaningful that I could do for the family.

I volunteered to combine our two Sunday school classes together for a while, so that Sharon would not have to be concerned with that responsibility. It was an opportunity for me to utilize some of the grief support training from Stephen Ministry to help the members of the classes. Additionally, it was an opportunity for the two classes to comfort and support each other in their grief. Personally, I was excited to be given this chance to be God's hands and feet in such a difficult and unusual situation.

As I prepared for the first Sunday that the classes were to be combined the Lord led me to the above passage of Scripture from 2 Timothy. The verses describe Paul's condition as he was awaiting the end of his ministry on Earth. As I read the verses, I realized that they also applied to Robert's life, in the following paraphrased form:

> He was being poured out as a drink offering in Iraq
> His time of departure was at hand, as he was traveling
> in the Military convoy on that April day with six
> other men
> He had fought the good fight with his fellow soldiers
> It was his time for finishing the race
> He had kept his faith throughout the years through
> this day
> Ahead of him is laid up the crown of righteousness
> That the Lord, the Righteous Judge, will give to
> Robert today
> And not only will the Lord give a crown to Robert, but
> He will also give it to all other believers who
> Have loved the Lord! 2 Timothy 4:6-8 NASB

Our God! Six years later I would have still chosen the same verses to focus the lesson upon. Recently I opened my Bible to find those marked verses. How awesome is our God.

Fortunately, we don't have to face the reality of a wartime death story like our hero Robert on a regular basis. But, we need to think about the verses from the end of Paul's life and how our life's journey reflects upon those verses. Would we be able to paraphrase the verses from *2Timothy 4:6-8* NASB and apply them to ourselves, as I have done with Robert's life?

Robert's legacy continues to live on, through the life of his mother Sharon and his father Deacon. Both of his parents mentor young men and women entering the military life at West Point. They continue to be involved with the high school athletic programs at Sandy Creek High School, Robert's alma mater. A scholarship fund has been awarded every year, for the past ten years, with the motto of "Not by ability, but by heart." Sharon continues to be known as "Mama Collins" by Robert's friends from West Point as they have married and started families of their own.

And remembering my daughter Janet's dreams for Robert, Sharon has spread her wings and gone on numerous mission trips here and abroad, doing the work that Robert probably would have enjoyed.

Having received the gifts of comfort and compassion from friends in Tyrone, the county of Fayette, the state of Georgia, the country of the United States, the US military, and countries abroad, Sharon and Deacon are truly examples of those who have received and then given back to others. Their humble spirit and love for others has taught all of us so very, very much. And we know that Robert will always be with us.

1 LT Robert W. Collins US Army stationed in Iraq. Last photo taken by his mother Ret. LT Col. Sharon Collins before deployment to Iraq.

CHAPTER 20

Protection in the Workplace

"For in the day of trouble He will keep me safe in His dwelling; He will hide me in the shelter of His tabernacle and set me high upon a rock. Then my head will be exalted above the enemies who surround me; at his tabernacle will I sacrifice with shouts of joy; I will sing and make music to the LORD."

Psalm 27:5-6 NIV

One night when I wasn't able to sleep, I turned the TV on to my favorite middle of the night fare "Reflections." It is a show that combines scenes of the outdoors, soothing music which is mostly sacred in tone, and streaming verses of Scripture. Ever since I have been sick with the Giant Cell Arteritis, I have spent many hours watching this show.

My routine is to have one of my Bibles in hand, along with a pen to mark whatever I hear God speaking to me about. Sometimes a particular verse may really grab my attention and I will spend quite a bit of time "reflecting" upon it. I may even read the surrounding scripture and study notes in my Bible.

With the writing of this book, I had not really thought about including God's mercy and comforting Grace with respect to my work experience. However, when a particular verse appeared on the TV screen, I heard God speaking loudly and clearly to me. I spent the remainder of the night studying the surrounding Scriptures and researching some related verses. An outline of events related to my working career tumbled out onto a sheet of paper. The facts, that it had been twenty-four years since I had worked, and forty-nine years since I had started working, didn't matter. God had a message He wanted me to share with others.

The first thoughts that came to my mind, when I read the above Scripture on the TV, were related to something that happened just a few years ago, long after I had to quit working. I realized on the day when the event happened that God was still protecting me in my career, even though the "active" phase was completed.

An Unexpected Visitor

Several months after I had been diagnosed with Giant Cell Arteritis, the doorbell rang at our front door. We very seldom have anyone come to our front door – maybe once every couple months. So, it is usually with caution that we open that door. Jim went to the door and spoke briefly with the individual. Then he had the man come inside the house and had me come join both of them.

At this point in time, I knew that God was providing me protection, for many reasons.

My husband was at home, rather than off working or running errands.

I have always been very cautious about being left alone with a stranger. Without Jim's presence, I certainly would have been vulnerable in my own home.

This man appeared at our house without any notice beforehand, whatsoever. He had traveled over a thousand miles to question me and he didn't even know if I would be at home.

The man knew a lot about me and my business relationships.

Jim was aware of my working relationships and therefore was able to help me answer the man's questions.

I was on 40 mg of prednisone a day, along with methotrexate. Accordingly, I was not able to think and comprehend as was normal for me. This is often referred to as "brain fog."

The tone of the conversation with the man quickly became very serious and overwhelming. Fortunately, we had seated ourselves where Jim and I could have eye contact with each other. Suffering with the discomfort of the illness and my weakened condition, the situation at hand was almost more than I could handle. But, I quickly sent silent prayers to my Heavenly Father for His protection. I realized that **I could possibly be implicated in the situation at hand and that every word I spoke was crucial**. Some of the beginning questions were:

- Did I know where a certain person was?
- When was the last time I had contact with that person?
- What kind of work had I done with that person and others?
- Had I worked on such and such projects?
- Had I traveled to certain places?
- Questions about the person's personal life?
- Did I know who other people were?

The questions continued for several hours, digging deeper and deeper into details, searching for information that was pertinent both from national and international perspectives. I was spent emotionally and physically exhausted. **This interrogation was beyond anything I had ever been through during the active part of my career**. However, I realized what the legal ramifications were and which foreign courts were involved. It was nothing to mess around with!

Because of the legal sensitivity of this situation, I am not at liberty to discuss it any further. What I can tell you is that we **never know what to expect, what will come out of the woodwork, when it will come,** or what type of clothing it will come in. The **enemy is always on the prowl**, ready to devour us, when we least expect it. That is why we always should have the Armor of God covering us, ready for whatever battle comes our way.

In the above Scripture, God is offering us His protection in His Sanctuary. **What holier place is there than God's Sanctuary?** This verse comes from the Psalms in the Old Testament and is based on the concept of God and the Temple with its Holy of Holies. God was protecting me from my enemies and placing me high on a rock. It is no wonder that when I saw those two verses on the TV screen, I thought of the day that investigator came to our home. My heart was filled with thanksgiving as I realized the connection between the Scripture and the event. Yes, there has been more activity since that day, but I know who my Protector is and will be.

The Armor of God

In Ephesians, Paul instructs the people about wearing the Armor of God to protect themselves, which I referred to above.

"Finally be strong in the Lord and in His mighty power. Put on the full armor of God so that you can **take your stand against the devil's schemes**. For our struggle is not against flesh and blood, but against the rulers, against the authorities, against the powers of this dark world and against the spiritual forces of evil in the heavenly realms. Therefore put on the full armor of God, so that when the day of evil comes, you may be able to stand your ground, … Stand firm then, with the **belt of truth buckled around your waist,** with the **breastplate of righteousness** in place, and with your **feet** fitted with the readiness that comes from the **gospel of peace**. In addition to all this, take up the **shield of faith**, with which you can extinguish all the flaming arrows of the evil one. Take the **helmet of salvation** and the **sword of the Spirit**, which is the **word of God**. And **pray in the Spirit** on all occasions with all kinds of prayers and requests. With this in mind, be alert and always keep on praying for all the saints." Eph 6:10-18 NIV

The above story is not what I had expected to be the ending events to my accounting career. Now I will return to the beginning of the twenty-five year journey that I traveled as a pioneer helping to open the frontier for other ladies to enter the field of professional accounting. That journey started almost fifty years ago, with much different technology and standards than exist today.

I certainly relied upon God's help as I dealt with personal challenges along the way. Additionally, my personal standards made the pathway even more stringent. This section contains a smattering of stories related to my work experience. It is not a resume of what my work experience was.

In another chapter of the book, I will discuss the abrupt ending to my career.

1966 – Working in a Man's World

When Jim and I got married, I needed to secure employment as soon as possible. With my degree in Economics and minor in Accounting, I knew it would be difficult to find employment in a market that was primarily male dominated. In 1966, most firms would not even consider interviewing a female for a professional position. Those were **the days before Equal Rights for women in the workplace.**

Eventually, I was hired by an international CPA firm Pannell, Kerr, Forster as a staff accountant. However, my opportunities would be limited, because I hired on with the understanding that I would not travel out of town. I quickly discovered that my personal attributes placed other limitations on my career.

- I was 22 years old
- I weighed about 100 pounds
- I was 4 foot 10 ½ inches tall
- I was shy and naïve
- I was not used to cussing and rough language
- I did not know about aggressive behavior from males in the workplace
- I was not experienced at traveling out of town by myself or with others
- I did not know how to stand up for myself.

In addition to working, I decided to earn my Master's degree at Georgia State University at night, taking one course at a time. At that pace, I would earn my Master of Professional Accountancy degree at the same time that Jim would complete his Bachelor's degree. Meanwhile, Jim went to Georgia State during the day to earn his Bachelor's degree in Accounting and worked at night at Western Union repairing teletype equipment as he had done while serving in the Air Force. Whew! It was a very busy schedule around our house and **not much time for being newlyweds!**

As I mentioned above, I quickly discovered that I had a major battle earning respect from the clients that I was assigned to serve. The first major hurdle was my appearance – no one wanted to take me seriously. I was young, petite in stature, and a female! I did learn though that **one of my strengths would be my "smile."** People had always commented about my smile and the way it radiated. So, I knew that I had to let my smile and dancing eyes open the doors to establish relationships with the clients.

Integrity was also important to me. Proverbs 10:9 has this to say about "integrity." "People with integrity have firm footing, but those who follow crooked paths will slip and fall." NLT

I never took being someone else's employee lightly. "Lazy people are a pain to their employer. They are like smoke in the eyes or vinegar that sets the teeth on edge." Proverbs 10:26 NLT

The lesson my parents preached over and over was honesty. In retrospect that probably prepared me "for The LORD hates cheating, but he delights in my career more than any other lessons. "in honesty." Proverbs 11:1 NLT

Proverbs 15:33 NLT states that, "Fear of the LORD teaches a person to be wise; humility precedes honor."

Proverbs 15:28 NLT "The godly think before speaking."

Pig Alley

Being shy and naïve as I was, I was fearful of being alone with men, in the clients' offices or buildings. I was not used to being in places like bars. I will never forget being given the assignment to observe inventory at the Pig Alley Bar, which was located down in the lower level of a building in a dark and secluded area of a building located on a side street in downtown Atlanta.

Much of the **inventory was placed in a room even further removed from safety**. The dank smell of the basement area, the odor of the booze, the cursing of the person taking inventory, and his off-color, sexist remarks were almost more than I could bear. And, to add to the mix, there was the rat that ran in front of me!

As time went on, I was given "more important" assignments. There were questions about fraud or misappropriations of income and expenses at one of the clients. I was mostly to observe and report on my observations, which I did. However, one Sunday I was driving by the client's business and observed some very important evidence which I reported.

A few days later, **I received a phone call from the client with a tirade of cussing coming over the phone lines,** while I was in another client's office. I was appalled at the behavior at the other end of the line. By this time, I had learned to be more assertive and stand up for myself. I politely asked him to cease talking to me that way, told him that his manner of talking was inappropriate, and that he could discuss the matter with the partner in charge at our office. This was a huge step for me. Although I did not recognize it at the time, God was providing me with His strength and kindness.

"The tongue of the wise commands knowledge, but the mouths of fools pour out folly." Prov. 15:2 ESV

Proverbs 17:12 NLT "It is safer to meet a bear robbed of her cubs than to confront a fool caught in folly."

My Mentor

Early in my employment I was assigned to work with one company that had many locations and they were based in Atlanta. Since I had caveated my employment that I would not travel, I spent much time in their offices. It was in this environment that God granted me His compassion and grace in training me for my career in public accounting. The owner of the business respected me for who I was. **It didn't matter that I was a female**, because his chief personal financial assistant was a woman whom he highly respected. She and I quickly became professional equals and friends. Miss Hattie Carroll was my mentor. She taught me self-confidence and self-respect. We were friends and business associates until the end of my career. I will forever be indebted to her. She was God's gift to me!

If you think about it, all of us have had certain persons who have been instrumental in helping us achieve success in our working careers. Some have taught us working skills, others have taught us life skills. Some have been there to comfort us in our times of need and there have been times when we have been called upon to show compassion to others. That is one of God's provisions for us.

Prov 12:25 NLT "…an encouraging word cheers a person up."

Prov13:20 NLT "Whoever walks with the wise will become wise; whoever walks with fools will suffer harm."

Mentoring to Others

After I had Janet and Ricky, I worked on a consulting basis for some of the same clients that I had worked for through the CPA firm. Eventually, I established my own CPA and consulting firm.

One of the services that I offered to clients was bookkeeping training and education, as well as the same for computerized accounting systems. I also taught adult education classes in community school programs, teaching the students how to use accounting software programs. **Teaching was always very rewarding to me, as I used my imagination** to engage the students in meaningful dialogues to help them learn.

Proverbs 16:21 NLT "The wise are known for their understanding, and instruction is appreciated if it's well presented."

Proverbs 16: 24 NLT "Kind words are like honey – sweet to the soul and healthy for the body."

I was blessed time and again to have opportunities to share my faith in our Lord with people in the workplace settings. Generally, people knew where I stood with my faith and respected me with their actions. However, as I am sure most of you have experienced, there were times when certain individuals mocked my faith or exhibited inappropriate behavior in front of me. I would be remiss if I did not admit that there were times that I did not stand up for Jesus whole-heartedly as I should have. My heart grieves for the sins I committed that way.

I will never forget the young lady who was **struggling with certain life events and also the concept of a spiritual life.** I had been doing consulting work in her office for some time and we had established a relationship that allowed for in depth discussions. One night about 3:00 in the morning, our phone rang, startling me awake from my deep sleep. She was very emotional and needed help right away. She was struggling, trying to put salvation and believing in Jesus all together. We spent time sorting through her confusion, clearing her tears, and calming her anxiety. Later that morning she gave her heart to Jesus. Once again tears flowed down her face, but they were the sweet tears of God's love.

"For God so loved the world that He gave His only Son, that whosoever believed in Him should not perish, but have everlasting life." John 3:16 NASB

Tax Returns for the Elderly

One of the things that I enjoyed was serving a group of elderly citizens during tax season. I never really made any money during this time – it was **a ministry of sorts**. I would go to their houses and pick up their information and then return the completed tax returns to their houses. I would easily spend hours coming and going, visiting with them, listening to their stories of what had happened during the last year. I would comfort them, cry with them, smile with them, and make suggestions to them. It was sad when there were deaths or major illnesses. God had me doing this ministry to spread His comforting Grace.

"It is possible to give freely and become more wealthy, but those who are stingy will lose everything." Proverbs 11:24 NLT

Ice and Snow

After Cynthia was born in April, I returned to working in January, when she was nine months old. We left her with a new baby sitter Cheryl Dunn Cross, who lived in Fayetteville. The day was very cold and blustery, with some prospects of snow, but not until late in the day. However, about four o'clock in the afternoon, the snow came in like a blizzard. Quickly the streets became covered. In 1981, in Atlanta, preparations for clearing snow were not a high priority. As the temperatures dropped, the snow on the streets turned into ice. On that day, Jim and I were both working in downtown Atlanta, so we had driven only one car into the city.

I walked up to his office and we went to the parking lot to get the car. It took us an hour to slip and slide out of the surface lot and around one city block. By this time, it was dark. The radio reports were saying that the expressways were already at a standstill with lots of accidents. The highways in Fayetteville, where we lived, were shut down by the police. We knew that we couldn't get home. So, we drove back into the surface parking lot that we had just left an hour ago.

We walked back to Jim's office and prepared to spend the night in one of the high rise office buildings on Peachtree Street in Peachtree Center, Atlanta. But, first we had to make some kind of arrangements about Cynthia and our two older children. Janet and Ricky had gotten home from school safely and one of the neighbors had already taken them in to spend the night. Cell phones were not part of our life at this time, so we had to use the phones in Jim's office.

However, what were we going to do about our baby Cynthia? Today had been her first day at Cheryl's! How could we ask Cheryl to take care of her tonight? Cynthia would probably cry all night. We called Cheryl and she quickly volunteered to keep Cynthia, stating that it wasn't safe to drive her to our neighbor's where Janet and Ricky were staying. Cheryl reached out and comforted us in our anxiety. **God provided for our needs in this most unexpected circumstance of a major ice and snowstorm.** The next day we heard stories of the wonderful time that they shared, including having home-made pancakes.

Why do I include this story? **Child care** is a very important consideration with most families in conjunction with their employment. There will always be those stories of unforeseen circumstances. This is just one of ours. **How the situation is handled, with compassion and comforting grace, can dictate how the family unit exits the event.**

"A prudent person foresees the danger ahead and takes precautions; the simpleton goes blindly on and suffers the consequences." Proverbs 22:3 NLT

Cheryl's taking care of Cynthia that night reminds me of the Scripture in *2 Corinthians 9:8-10 NLT.*

"And God will generously provide all you need. Then you will always have everything you need and plenty left over to share with others. As the Scriptures say,

"Godly people give generously to the poor." 2 Cor 11:7-8 NLT

Their good deeds will never be forgotten." 2 Cor 11:11 NLT

For God is the one who gives seed to the farmer and then bread to eat. In the same way, He will give you many opportunities to do good, and He will produce a great harvest of generosity in you." 2 Cor 9:10 NLT I have seen this group of verses in action. Have you?

Changes

From the time that I started working in 1966, until my career was abruptly ended in 1991, many changes occurred for women working in the field of professional accounting. In many respects, **I was one of the pioneers opening the doors** for young ladies to pursue careers in future years. Eventually, many of the major CPA firms had to take pro–active measures to hire men to fulfill certain staff positions, because women had started dominating the numbers of positions filled.

In the private sector of industry and in governmental and institutional positions, women have also proven their abilities and been hired in key positions. When I was pursuing my undergraduate degree in Economics, I was one of a few female students involved in that given field. It was a likewise scenario, when I earned my Master's degree in Professional Accountancy.

As I have reflected over my career, I give the glory to God for the gifts that He gave me. Also, I am thankful for the strength and wisdom He provided to face the challenges of each day as I matured in the process of earning my CPA certification and the ability to own my own business.

My last years of working were spent as a partner in a small investment banking firm. It was the **highlight of my career, the culmination of all the skills** that I had developed over the years, and the opportunity to expand into new areas. I enjoyed the excitement of working with clients in helping them raise funds to expand their businesses. Creating the offering documents, including the financial projections and written documentation, was a totally new challenge.

Some Family Support

I think back to the time when my daddy was the treasurer at our newly formed United Methodist Church in Satellite Beach, Florida. He helped me learn to keep the church's journals and ledgers in the pen and ink system that was used in the 1960's. That was the beginning of my accounting career....before I went to college and studied economics and accounting.

My Gramps Conklin kept books for many businesses. His **business sense and detailed oriented ways were naturals for me**. As a child, I didn't appreciate what he did, but I did in later years.

And, then there was Jim's Aunt Clio. She was **my encourager**, always letting me know that with God's help I could complete my Master's degree, pass the CPA exam, and make it in the male-dominated work place. When I was discouraged, she comforted me with God's love and grace. She quoted Scripture to me. And she loved me.

Choices?

Over the years, I worked with many different clients and on numerous occasions they offered me permanent employment with their companies. Yes, there were times when it was tempting to consider their offers, but I always said "no" until the last couple years of my career.

The primary reason that I said "no" was that I felt too often that there **would be a compromising of my Christian beliefs and the ethics** of a Certified Public Accountant with the demands of a particular potential employer. As I had worked with these clients, I could foresee that there might be times when they would be tempted to push me to act in certain ways that I would not feel comfortable with. Have you ever felt that way?

Perhaps I harbored certain fears that I was not strong enough to stand up to these potential employers in the same way that I was able to do so, as an independent contractor. Maybe I needed to be able to trust God more completely. Then again, maybe my saying "no" to being hired by these companies, kept them respecting my decisions and abiding by what needed to be done.

A passage of Scripture addresses this very issue.

"But remember that the temptations that come into your life are no different from what others experience. And God is faithful. He will keep the temptation from becoming so strong that you can't stand up against it. When you are tempted, he will show you a way out so that you will not give in to it." I Cor 10:13 NLT

Whatever our individual choices are − being an employee or independent − it is our responsibility to conduct ourselves in a Godly manner and to show compassion to others in the workplace. My father spent his last working years working in the Space Industry, as a supervisor with Pan Am Services. His mother, my Grandma Conklin wrote him a letter, part of which I am quoting. I can well imagine her writing the same to me, encouraging me in the field of Certified Public Accountants.

> **"Work with enthusiasm,**
> **As though you were working**
> **For the Lord**
> **Rather than for people." Ephesians 6:7 NLT**

Bette working on an individual tax return.

CHAPTER 21

At Noon on a Monday

It was noon on a Monday, the fourth of February, 1991. I was leaving Fayetteville, headed to a client's office in Atlanta. I pulled up to a major intersection and stopped for the traffic light. In the next moment, I heard metal type noises, felt an intense electrical type shock all the way to the top of my head, felt a jarring movement, and sensed that something was terribly wrong, but I didn't know what. Then,,,,,,, I realized that I had been hit from behind by another vehicle.

That vehicle was a heavy-duty Chevrolet pickup truck, with a winch or towing type device on the front end of it. The extended device had caught my car from underneath and jerked it around. Kind of like a dog shaking a toy. That in turn had caused my body to receive the force of the accident, leaving my car virtually undamaged.

The driver of the pickup had not stopped for the traffic light and had hit my car in the process. He left the scene of the accident, but I was able to get his vehicle tag number. I reported it to the police. They recognized his vehicle and tag number. So, they drove to the nearby concrete plant where he worked. They found and investigated him. He was drunk at 2.4, or three times the legal alcohol limit…at noon on a Monday.

It was not a pretty scene when the police brought him back to the scene of the accident. Because of his drunken state, he had a wild story to tell and was very disrespectful towards me. I was shocked at his drunken state at noon on a Monday. I had always thought that accidents like this happened on Friday and Saturday nights.

Later that afternoon, I went to the local urgent care center because of the pain in my neck and back and an accompanying headache. After X-rays and an exam, the doctor re-assured me that with a few days of rest and some medicine, I would be fine. He said it was, "**Just some whiplash**." I waited patiently, but the pain and discomfort didn't disappear. In fact, it seemed to get worse and it also moved down into my left arm. I had several appointments with a neurologist over the next two months and I kept being told to **be patient and I would be ok**.

Finally, at the end of March an MRI was scheduled. In 1991 CT scans and MRI's were not done as easily or frequently as they are done today. Having the MRI done was one of the most painful and exhausting experiences of my life.

The next day, I received a call that I **needed to be seen by a neurosurgeon right away.** At that appointment, I was told that with any wrong movement, I could become a **quadriplegic**. What that meant was that "I could become paralyzed from the neck down the rest of my body and lose control of all movement from the neck downward." That was a very, very scary thought. And, it also explained why I was in so much pain.

The following week, a lengthy and complex operation was performed to allow the spinal column in my neck to return from a flattened shape, back to its natural, round shape. Bone was taken from my left hip to fuse the fourth, fifth, and sixth vertebrae into one long vertebra. I have never fully recovered from the pain in my neck. The post-op period was extremely difficult physically and emotionally. Even today, movement of my neck is limited because of the way the vertebrae have been fused together.

It wasn't until November that the doctors recognized that part of the pain I was continuing to experience was related to my left shoulder. The **upper part my arm had been shoved up into the shoulder joint. It was not in its proper place and as a result was impinged**. It took two surgeries to relieve some of that displacement. After the second of those surgeries, I had to travel every day to physical therapy for two weeks, including Thanksgiving Day. The drive was 30 miles each direction. Finding a ride for each day was not an easy task. At that time, **physical therapy was not available in our local area.**

After continuing therapy and other methods of trying to improve my pain and discomfort, I was **finally diagnosed with fibromyalgia (fibro)**. My case of fibro was attributed to the long-term effects of the injuries from the accident and its related stress. At that time, most doctors and health practioners did not recognize fibromyalgia. Often it was referred to as a "trash can" diagnosis. In reality, what it meant was that I had an **"invisible" disease that many people questioned and I was living with the stigma of that**. In addition, people did not understand why my neck fusion was not healing properly. Talk about frustration.

The other component that set in after the accident was a deep depression. Having worked in the professional field of accounting and practiced as a Certified Public Accountant with national firms and then establishing my own firm, I was very professional and particular about the way that I worked.

Prior to the accident, I had worked with an investment banking firm, which was very demanding professionally and presentation-wise. Everything was measured against the **standard of "Perfection."** Everything was either black or white. Nothing could be gray. There were no exceptions to the rules. My work was subject to the standards of the American Institute of CPA's (AICPA) and Peer Review. And in the investment banking world my work was also subject to the standards of the Securities and Exchange Commission (SEC) and all of the related licensing with those governmental agencies.

I took everything about my work very seriously to the nth degree. This was nothing new for me, because as a child and a teen-ager, that was the way that I was expected to do my school work and household chores.

CHAPTER 22

I Didn't Know Ministers Wrote Prescriptions (Rx)

Thinking back to my story about our engagement and how I wrote about Jim's plans for God to be first in our marriage, I'm sure some of you had some other thoughts about those statements. I also wrote that if it had not been for our faith and friends we probably would not have persevered through the years. This all leads to a story that I didn't expect to happen. **I can only remember within a ten-year range when it happened, but I recall the lesson very vividly.**

For some reason the closeness in our marriage had disappeared. We weren't happy. No matter what the subject was, Jim was on one end of the balance and I was on the other end. **And the kids were out there, hanging somewhere by themselves, wondering what on earth Mom and Dad were doing**. It's a wonder they survived!

Jim went to work. I went to work. We either argued or avoided each other at other times. **It got where I couldn't stand it any longer. I tried to hide it at work. Some days I went to work so tired I could hardly function.**

Fortunately, I did consulting work and one day I decided I just had to leave the client's office. I couldn't stay another minute. I called a former pastor of ours and asked if I could come and see him. A half hour later I was in his office, trying to tell him about our unhappiness. He and Jim were much closer friends than I, since they attended sporting events together. I felt like I was at a disadvantage, but I still trusted his wisdom and judgment. As I write this, I cannot remember the source of all the unhappiness.

All I knew was that my marriage was at a breaking point and I had to do something about it. I knew that God was in charge and I needed to turn the problem over to Him. However, with all the discord going on, that wasn't easy to do. My faith wasn't at its strongest at this point in time. I had to swallow my pride and go to someone for help. That wasn't my normal mode of operation! And I certainly wasn't going to let Jim know that I was going to go and talk to his friend Bob about our situation.

Once again God's compassion flowed through one of His faithful servants, as our former pastor ministered to me. He listened patiently to me for a short while, not taking in many details, nor listening to many accusations for he loved both of us. Then he pulled out a sheet of paper and he said to me, "**Bette, I am going to write out a prescription for you and Jim. You and Jim are both to pray together about this situation.**"

That was twenty-five or more years ago, who knows. It doesn't matter. What matters is that I have recalled that prescription many times through the years. It has been **like a comforting balm for my soul and life.**

The source material for anyone facing this situation is the book of Proverbs in the Old Testament of the Bible. It is filled with advice for anyone willing to take the time to read and study its contents. I highly recommend regular study of Proverbs for anyone on a regular basis. Following is an assortment of verses that I have randomly chosen to include in this chapter for you to read. They progress from giving advice to family living.

- , Prov13:13 NLT "People who despise advice will find themselves in trouble; but those who respect it, we will succeed."
- Prov14:1NLT "A wise woman builds her house; a foolish woman tears hers down with her own hands."
- Prov15:1, 7 NLT "A gentle answer turns away wrath, but harsh words stir up anger." "Only the wise can give good advice, fools cannot do so." V.32 If you reject criticism, you only harm yourself, but **if you listen to correction, you grow in understanding."** V.33 "Fear of the LORD teaches a person to be wise; humility precedes honor." V.16 "It is better to have fear for the LORD than to have great treasure with turmoil." v.3 "Gentle words bring life and health; a deceitful tongue crushes the spirit."
- Prov 21:9 NLT "It is better to live alone in the corner of an attic than with a **contentious wife in a lovely home**."
- Prov 21:19 NLT "It is better to live alone in the desert than with a **crabby, complaining wife**. The wise have wealth and luxury, but fools spend whatever they get."
- Prov 21:15 NLT "**Justice is joy** to the godly, but it causes dismay among the evildoers."

CHAPTER 23

Reconnecting at the Lincoln Memorial "Lord, Have Mercy on Me!"

To be completely honest, after my daddy died, my mother and I were not compatible with each other as my father had wished we would be. Remember in the story "An Early Death" that he had given me instructions about her right before his heart surgery, regarding our future relationship. He had been right in sensing that we might have difficulties. Mom and I had differences in opinions regarding certain social issues and business matters with respect to her personal life. Accordingly, it affected our relationship. That bothered me. **Wanting to set a good example for my own daughters, I decided I needed to do something about it**.

I knew that she liked to travel and had not done much traveling since daddy died. So, I decided, a vacation might be a good thing for her. I did some research into places to visit where she and I could go together comfortably and have a relatively good time.

Thinking back over family vacations with Mom, Daddy, and Lois and I, Washington DC came to mind as a possibility. Jim and I had taken a few short trips there and thoroughly enjoyed them. A longer trip with Mom might work. So, I called her and asked if she would like to take a vacation with me to Washington, DC and Williamsburg, VA and do lots of sight-seeing. She had been to those areas with her Eastern Star groups and had enjoyed them and accordingly was receptive.

Putting aside our silent warfare, she told me to make plans and let her know what we were going to do and when. Now I had to please the "perfection" person.

She made some requests of things to do, including going to Senator Bill Nelson's office and arranging for a tour of the White House and Capitol Building through their staffs. I had gone to Melbourne High School in Melbourne, Florida with Bill Nelson and **knew Senator Nelson from our classes. Since he was her Senator, she wanted to take advantage of those connections**. Surprisingly, I was successful in arranging the requested tours through Bill's office and that **put Mom in a positive mood for the trip.**

I researched the other sites in DC and set up an itinerary for us. I also made plans for seeing Jamestown and its recent renovations after some hurricane damage. She was tickled when we went to the statue of Pocahontas and I took a **photo of her and Pocahontas holding hands**. The day we did the Senate tour, we had our photo made with Senator Nelson. These **little extra jesters of paying attention to her went a long way**. She loved the individual attention and she then transferred it to our relationship with each other.

As I mentioned in another story, she was somewhat skittish and fearful of some things. **Those fears raised their ugly heads when it came to walking across some of the busy streets.**

On one occasion, she completely froze up and after getting her feet into the street, she was unable to continue walking. That brought the surrounding traffic to a complete stop. Drivers of the cars could not proceed with driving and had to come to complete stops on main streets in central, downtown Washington, DC because of her fears. **I was forced to coax her to relax and put her fears aside and let me be in charge.** Eventually, she was able to put one foot in front of the other and move across the main thorough fare. Whew! What a challenge! She let me be in charge of getting from point A to point B. The remainder of our day progressed nicely.

Later we went to the Lincoln Memorial, parking the car in the Handicap area. While on the trip, I had brought some of my Praise and Worship CD's to play to entertain me and provide intervention music. Mom was not a person who enjoyed that type of music and vocalized her opinion about such. Accordingly, I had to carefully choose when I played the CD's, so as to not aggravate her, with their sound.

When we got into the car after seeing the Lincoln Memorial, our plans were to drive to the National Cathedral, during the five o'clock rush hour in DC. Getting out of the parking space was not easy with the heavy foot traffic around us, along with the hundreds of cars leaving the city. I pondered which direction to go and was flustered.

Without thinking, I punched the dial and put the CD player on. Uh, oh! Mom was going to get upset with the NOISE and traffic. The song **"Lord, have mercy on me" started playing. Immediately, I started laughing. With her limited hearing, she asked what I was laughing at. I told her about the words to the song. Asking the Lord to have "mercy on me". All of a sudden, she forgot her dislike of Praise and Worship music and she laughed.** And I could hear God laughing, too.

The turns to go from the Lincoln Memorial to the National Cathedral are tricky and I made some errors. We ended up on the loops to the Jefferson Memorial and the beautiful water ponds surrounding it. Once more I started singing out, "Lord, have mercy on me." And, **my singing is pretty BAD.**

The time had come for mom and me to reconnect and our relationship to heal. All because of a Praise and Worship song, heavy traffic in DC, and my bad singing. And giving it all to Jesus. See what you can do to heal family relationships and enjoy the future years together. It's worth it. We celebrated her ninetieth birthday, did some other vacations together, spent her dying hours together, talked on the phone a lot, did grandparenting together, and got her ready to go to Heaven to be with Boppa (my daddy) after forty years of being a widow. Yes, "Mercy" is a wonderful gift from the Lord for his children.

Take time and mend those problems. It's worth it. For almost two weeks, mom was more dependent upon me than she normally was; she needed assistance with everyday activities; she needed **mercy** with her way of doing things; and enjoying the trip.

I needed **mercy** to accept the responsibility of taking care of my mom who was in her eighties and handicapped with hearing and vision losses and afraid of venturing out. I needed patience to be holy and kind after convincing her to go on a vacation. I needed to be able to adhere to a passage of Scripture from the book of Colossians to show her holiness in a Christ-like manner, so that she could feel Compassion and know that I really loved her.

So put to death the sinful, earthly things lurking within you. Have nothing to do with sexual sin, impurity, lust, and shameful desires. Don't be greedy for the good things of this life, for that and idolatry. God's terrible anger will come upon those who do such things. Get rid of anger, rage, malicious behavior, slander and dirty language. Don't lie to each other, for you have stripped off your old evil nature and all its wicked deeds. In its place you have clothed yourselves with a brand new nature that is continually being renewed as you learn more and more about Christ who created this new nature within you.............Since God choose you to be the holy people, whom he loves, you must clothe yourselves with tenderhearted mercy, kindness, humility, gentleness, and patience. You must make allowances for each other's faults and forgive the person who offends you. Remember the Lord forgave you, so you must forgive others. And the most important piece of clothing you must wear is love. Love is what binds us all together in perfect harmony. And let the peace that come from Christ rule in your heads. For as members of one body, you are all called to live in peace. And always be thankful." Colossians 3:5-15 NLT. Mercy and love are spoken of together in the same passage of Scripture.

Mom, Lorraine Conklin (d) holding hand of Pocahontas at Jamestown, VA 10/14/05. Restoration tent in background.

Mom, Lorraine Conklin(d) and Bette with Bette's former classmate from Melbourne High School and Florida Senator Bill Nelson in the Senate Office Building. Bill had just given us an update on an active hurricane headed for the area where mom lived in Florida.

Lincoln Memorial statue of the President of the United States in this impressive memorial to him. It was at this setting that mom and I began our reconciliation.

CHAPTER 24

Gifts from the Holy Land

For well over a hundred and twenty-five years, the Statue of Liberty in New York City's Harbor has been one of the world's most beloved monuments. The Statue is a **symbol that brings comfort and a feeling of security to people whenever they see it**. In fact, the feelings may be evoked even through photographs, postage stamps, miniature statues or other reproductions. As people have come to the United States as immigrants, the Statue of Liberty was the one thing they were looking forward to viewing, knowing that they had reached their destination. It was a source of comfort to their souls. In today's society, as people travel in and out of New York City or in and out of the USA, the Statue of Liberty represents the "comfort" of their homeland.

Likewise, in our great land, there are other locations or **monuments that stir people's emotions and bring comfort to**

their souls or needs. For the western part of our country, I think of the Golden Gate Bridge in San Francisco Bay. For the Mid-West, one may think of the Arch in St. Louis, along side the mighty Mississippi River. In the Black Hills of South Dakota, Mount Rushmore with its presidential portraits carved into the mountainside might bring a feeling of security to its viewer. Washington, DC is filled with visual monuments galore, ready to bring comfort to all who come to visit this wondrous city.

Then, there are the gardens and **parks that may bring solace to many individuals as they reach out to have their needs met.** Here they may do so by themselves or in harmony with another individual of group of people. I think of my granddaughter Kaley who thoroughly enjoyed herself and found a sense of comfort when we were in Washington, DC in the Mall area near the Reflection Pond in front of the Lincoln Memorial. As a free spirit, she chased a squirrel around the grounds for nearly a half hour. She laughed and did her own thing. And, she enjoyed having us watch her have fun. Why was this important? She was dealing with the sadness of her parents' divorce and **here she was free from her feelings**.

A short while later Kaley and her younger sister Abby observed a memorial service at the new World War II Monument. Their attention was thoroughly captured as they watched the elderly veterans honor those of their unit who had died in combat. Kaley and Abby loved the pageantry of the uniforms, hats, gloves, and the beautiful wreath adorned in patriotic colors, accompanied by the music. They felt the compassion of the group gathered together celebrating those who had given the ultimate sacrifice of their individual lives.

Once the service was completed, the girls gathered with their mother and me to finish processing their feelings over this new life experience. We sat together by the calming pools of water at the World War II Monument and talked about the soldiers and the significance of the ceremony. It was time for them to have a lesson in compassion at the tender ages of seven and eight. Afterwards, they decided to dance together in the pools of water, expressing their feelings about the experience in their own way. Compassion was being expressed in the visual, the artistic, and with feelings. Learning about the day's activities by reading or hearing, just would not have been the same!

Most of us have a **favorite painting or photograph that hangs on the wall** in our home or in a relative's home. There is something comforting when we see that particular scene or person in the given artwork. Sometimes the piece of art **may be passed down from generation to generation**. In our home, that painting hangs in our living room. It is an oil painting of the favorite local attraction Starr's Mill in Brooks, Georgia, a grain mill and water fall. The painting was created by one of my former tax clients Nathan Mathews, who later authorized the reproduction of one hundred lithographs of the original. My husband was given permission to purchase the original to hang in his corporate office of United Parking in downtown Atlanta and later allowed to bring to our home. Our youngest daughter recently stated that is **one thing we will have to "duke it out"** over when **Mom and Dad pass on**. Its calming nature is special to our children, along with personal memories of the actual Starr's Mill.

Some people may have a **favorite piece of artwork**, such as a handmade vase, that brings them comfort because of what it represents or who gave it to them. I have several pieces of **jewelry that are special** to me, because of the times and reasons that my husband Jim gave them to me. Accordingly, I wear them at certain times, when I want to feel that **he is close to me** and that I am being comforted by my dear husband.

I have presented all of this discussion to point out that **we are able to be comforted in our needs by the visual dimension.** Granted, in most of our thinking, we relate to interpersonal reactions, but I would like you to think of other dimensions of comforting others. **Use your imagination** to discover how you may serve the Lord in showing His compassion to others.....through the visual, hearing, touching or other sensory dimensions.

In our home we have **four special gifts that we have received from friends who have had the opportunity to travel to** the **Holy Land**. I cherish each of these gifts as a form of God's comforting grace that is ever present in our home. These four items, through the visual dimension, minister to us in many different ways, through their silent voices.

The Mezuzah

The first item that we received was a Mezuzah. I can just hear you now, "What on earth is that? I have never seen that word or even heard of such a thing." At one time, I would have said the same thing. It is the parchment upon which Hebrew words from the Torah or Old Testament, primarily from Deuteronomy, are written. The Mezuzah is placed in a small wooden receptacle that is nailed to the wall of the home, outside of a door frame. The container that was given to us is made of olive wood, with a metal embossed flame placed on the front side. In the Bible or the Torah, **God instructs His people to place His word on the doorframes of their houses or the gates**. The Scripture below, in bold print is a section of familiar verses to most believers. This passage is referred to as the Shema.

The Shema **"Hear, O Israel: The LORD our God, the LORD is one. Love the LORD your God with all your heart and with all your soul and with all your strength. These commandments that I give you today are to be upon your hearts. Impress them on your children. Talk about them when you sit at home and when you walk along the road, when you lie down and when you get up. Tie them as symbols on your hands and bind them on your foreheads. Write them on the doorframes of your houses and on your gates."** Deuteronomy 6:4-9 NIV

Our mezuzah is placed by the door that enters the house from the garage, which is the entrance used most often. Accordingly, most people who enter our home are greeted with the Lord's Shema or a statement of our faith.

The Communion Cup

At the time of His last meal with His disciples, Jesus highlighted the body and the blood during the meal and explained their significance with respect to Himself and His life. The chalice or communion cup has become known as the visual image for the blood or wine and bread has become the image for Jesus' body. We were honored to receive a small communion cup, hand carved from the wood of an olive tree. It has been interesting to see the wood change in coloring as it has matured over the years.

What a precious gift to receive, this symbol representing **the blood, which washes away our sins, as God forgives our transgressions.** Truly this is a Gift of Compassion from the Lord.

"While they were eating, Jesus took some bread, and after a blessing, He broke it and gave it to the disciples, and said, 'Take, eat; this is My body.'

And when He had **taken a cup** and given thanks, He gave it to them, saying, '**Drink from it, all of you**;

For this is My **blood of the covenant**, which is poured out for many for **forgiveness of sins**.

But I say to you, I will not drink of this fruit of the vine from now on until that day when I drink it new with you in My Father's Kingdom.'" Matthew 26:26-29 NASB

The Nativity Scene

The single piece Nativity scene given to us is beautiful in its simplistic message of the birth of baby Jesus. Carved out of olive wood, the stable scene is complete with Mary, Joseph, and baby Jesus in a cradle. My friend Martha gave it to me as **a Christmas gift shortly after she returned from a quick trip to the Holy Land.**

I often think of her telling how she hurriedly looked through the display area in the retail shop at the airport trying to find three of what she wanted to have as gifts. She was a member of a Wednesday morning Bible study group of four women of which I was a part. I can just imagine Martha looking through the many items trying to find what she wanted, ever mindful that she only had a few minutes to complete her purchase. You see, she was about to miss her plane ride back to Atlanta from Israel. That causes me to **wonder further about how we sometimes put Jesus aside and then we scurry about and panic trying to find Him before our time runs out.**

Likewise, I think about the shepherds who looked for the baby Jesus after being told about Him by the Angels. Songs of adoration were sung by the Angels to announce His birth. Later the wise men followed the Star to come and worship the babe with their precious gifts. I wonder how the shepherds and wise men felt as they were traveling on their journeys to find baby Jesus.

When the angels had left them and gone into heaven, the shepherds said to one another. 'Let's go to Bethlehem and see this thing that has happened, which the LORD has told us about.'

Suddenly a great company of the heavenly host appeared with the angel, praising God and saying, Glory to God, in the Highest and on earth peace to men on whom his favor rests. Luke 2:13-14 NIV

So they hurried off and found Mary and Joseph, and the baby, who was lying in the manger." Luke 2:15-16 NIV

'...they will call Him Immanuel—which means, "God with us."' Matthew 1:23 NIV

How do we spend our time looking for Jesus? Are we serious about it?

Are we flippant about relating with Jesus?

How do we develop our relationship with Him?

Do we pick our relationship up, then put it down, feel guilty about it, pick it up again for a short while, and then hide it in a corner (of our mind or heart)? And, then...when life gets tough... do we panic...and say**...Jesus...where.... are...You?**

If **we shut the Lord out**, He has no opportunity to comfort us when we need His gifts of comfort and compassion.

A few years ago, Martha became very ill with several types of cancer and eventually died after treatment at Mayo Clinic in Jacksonville,

Florida. Throughout her journey, Martha and her husband Jim Watts' actions were recorded on Face book through "Martha's Journey to Victory". What a testimony Martha, Jim, and their friends presented to others as she traveled her journey to Heaven, unafraid, teaching all of us how to live graciously. **Now as I travel my journey, her faith journey of this nativity scene is a reminder of Martha's faith**. It had been my privilege to be Martha and Jim's Sunday school teacher for many years and to have Martha as a member of the Wednesday group that met at Joan's house for many years.

The group at Joan's was a group of women that I led in study of the Bible for approximately ten years every Wednesday morning. This group provided me with some of the deepest Bible study I ever knew. This gave me the spiritual base from which I drew upon during my greatest hours of despair during illness and after surgeries. Prayer was also an important component of this foursome group.

The Blue Mosaic Tile

The last gift is a round disc designed to look like a piece of mosaic tile, primarily with dark colored blue and white tiles. The tile is created to portray the story of the fishes and loaves, when Jesus fed the five thousand people by the Sea of Galilee, near Capernaum, in Israel. Two fishes and five loaves complete the design on the tile. Sometimes this Scripture lesson is known as the Lesson of Multiplication.

A crowd of 5,000 had gathered to hear Jesus speak and the disciples were concerned about feeding the crowd. Jesus had the disciples secure some fish and bread to feed the people and in the end, there was food left over. **How often do we doubt God's provision for our needs?** How often do we forget that **He knows our needs before we even verbalize them?** This story in the Bible is probably one of the most widely taught, but is it understood and believed as some of the other stories? Surely this is an example of God's providing comfort and compassion in time of need.

This pretty mosaic tile that my friend Airey gave me from her journey to Israel gives me plenty to think about with respect to my own life. I keep it in a safe and special place in my home, where I may see it on a regular basis.

"And He took the five loaves and the two fish and looking up toward Heaven, He blessed the food and broke the loaves and He kept giving them to the disciples to set before them; and He divided up the two fish among them all. They all ate and were satisfied."

We have been blessed to have these four gifts that are each so very different in nature and in their individual messages. Additionally, they all have a message of comfort that is unique and timeless for all of us.

Blue tile and Communion cup carved from olive wood from Israel received as gifts from friends who had traveled there.

**Nativity scene carved from olive wood from Israel received
as a gift from friends who had traveled there.**

The Twelve Stones

One of my favorite Bible stories is the Story of the Twelve Stones
from the Old Testament. At the end of the forty years of Moses
leading the children of Israel from their time of bondage in Egypt,
God told Moses that he would see the Promised Land, but he would
not pass into it. Joshua was appointed to lead the people into the land
that God had promised to Abraham and his descendants.

"And the children of Israel did so, just as Joshua commanded, and
took up twelve stones from the midst of the Jordan, as the LORD
had spoken to Joshua, according to the number of the tribes of the
children of Israel, and carried them over with them to the place
where they lodged, and laid them down there. Then Joshua set up
twelve stones in the midst of the Jordan, in the place where the feet

of the priests who bore the Ark of the Covenant stood, and they are there to this day." Joshua 4:8-9 NKJV

Previously, on their journey, God had parted the waters of the Red Sea for His children. Now, under Joshua's leadership, waters once again needed to be parted. **To commemorate this miraculous event and its spiritual significance, God had Joshua order the twelve tribes of Israel to gather up one stone for each tribe and place them together as a monument.** Additionally, God had Joshua gather up an additional twelve stones in the river where the Ark of the Covenant, the ark carrying the Holy of Holies, had been stationed in place as the people passed over the Jordan River.

Joshua then explained to the people that when their children asked about the stones, they were to tell them, when their children asked about the stones, they were to tell them, "Israel crossed over the riverbed. "So Joshua gave the command." Joshua then explained to the people that they crossed over the Jordan on dry land, for the LORD your God dried up the waters **of the Jordan before you until you had crossed over....that you may** fear the LORD your God forever." Joshua 4:21-24 NKJV

In His mighty wisdom, God had a monument created for the children of Israel to remember their entrance into the Promised Land and to recognize their fear of the Lord, their God forever. It is noteworthy that God had this done **immediately at the end of their journey and at the beginning of their occupancy of the Promised Land.** God also had a representative participate from each of the twelve tribes, so that it was an all-inclusive event. Once again, there was a visual image for the people to connect with God.

God's Gift of Visual Imagery

As I was writing about these visual gifts that God has given to us, He brought to my mind what I will term His Gift of Visual Imagery. We are so blessed to have the gift of eyesight and the resulting interpretation of the images by our brains.

Personally, I am a visual learner. **Visual images help me understand things that I might not understand otherwise. Perhaps you are the same way.** Reading about something in great detail from many different resources often is not the same as seeing a picture, drawing, or photograph of the subject at hand.

When I taught adult education computer classes, I utilized visual techniques to help the participants connect with developing their spreadsheets. In teaching my clients' staffs about their computer systems, I would develop everyday situations for them to identify with, so that they could then understand the "monster" computer system that was invading their space. I remember using the example of baking a cake from scratch to assist the students to be able to visualize the lesson via the comparable steps in making a cake.

You might say, "What does that have to do with comforting someone?" I say it has a lot to do with comforting them. Accordingly, I used lots of visual techniques for the following reasons:

1. Recognition of the **fact that the unknown** (what they were trying to learn) **was scary or difficult** to deal with.
2. Knocking fear of the unknown to a lower level of intensity was helpful.
3. Allowing for fun and laughter in the learning process puts people at ease.
4. Allowing for **group support of each other** in the learning environment.

The next time you see a friend or even a stranger struggling with putting something together or figuring out how to get on the next bus, think about **offering them a helping hand or words of encouragement.** There have been times when we have all gotten confused or lost and needed some direction or help. You have had to learn and be helped at one point in time and at some point it will be your turn to help others. Try using some of the visual techniques mentioned above in helping others. You just may be surprised at the outcome.

<u>Visual Reminders Bring Remembrance</u>

Now, what does this have to do with our lovely gifts from Israel? The Mezuzah, the Communion Cup, the Nativity Scene, and the Blue Mosaic Tile are all visual reminders of gifts of the Lord and His Comforting Grace for each one of us. Seeing each of these visual reminders brings to mind His love for us and the gift of His Son Jesus and everlasting life. The **visual reminders bring direction into our daily living, helping us seek His wisdom and guidance as we travel our individual journeys and then reach out to comfort others in their journeys.**

CHAPTER 25

Lab Visits and Sheep

No one likes to have their blood drawn at the lab, much less week after week after week. When I was **diagnosed with Giant Cell Arteritis, the autoimmune illness that attacked my arteries and veins,** I had to go to the local hospital to have blood tests done on a regular basis. In the beginning of my treatment with Prednisone and Methotrexate, I needed to go every week, and then every other week for months.

It just wasn't my favorite thing to do. I didn't feel like getting out of my pajamas and getting dressed to ride in the car for the few miles it took to get to the hospital lab. Besides, in the beginning months, it was the winter months and it was cold.

I didn't want to see anyone. I didn't want anyone to see how I looked. It didn't take long for me to take on the Prednisone look of Chippy Chipmunk, as I called myself. My face was chubby and swollen. My shoulders became hippopotamus humps. My belly was extra layers of steroid flab. I had forgotten what makeup was, because I just didn't want to be bothered with putting it on my red face. Jewelry – what was that?

Getting ready was an arduous task, but my sweet husband helped me get dressed. He was already proficient at putting on my socks and shoes from when I had a total knee replacement done the previous year. Patience was his middle name as he put on my coat and helped me out the door and into the car.

"God has given each of us the ability to do certain things well… if your gift is that of serving others, serve them well…And if you have a gift for showing kindness to others, do it gladly." Romans 12:6-8 NLT

Alfreda

Besides Jim's help, there was one other person who made this medical procedure bearable. It was Alfreda, the lab technician at the hospital. She made all the difference in the world for me and I know that **she makes a difference for a lot of other patients**, too. She never meets a stranger. She treats every patient as her friend. She cares about every patient and what they are going through with their illness or disease. She freely hands out hugs to the patients and their families.

Now when I go to the lab, it's not "I'm going to the lab." What I say is, "I get to go see Alfreda today!" If I'm not feeling well, she knows as soon as I walk into her room and she asks about it. If I'm down or sad, **she knows, by looking at my face**. And she asks. Alfreda has taught me much. Just as she offers compassion to others I have learned more skills about being compassionate to those I do not know.

Lambs, Sheep, and Shepherds

When you think of a lamb, what comes to your mind? A pure white sheep that is clean and neat in its appearance. Maybe a child's stuffed animal that they have received at Easter time. The playful lambs from the childhood rhyme "Mary had a little lamb." Generally, one thinks of something cuddly, warm, soft, or lovable.

However, when you think of a sheep, what comes to your mind? If you have lived on a farm or been around farm animals, you probably think of a dirty, smelly, bleating animal with a matted coat of wool. Sheep keep their heads to the ground looking for the next tuft of grass to graze on and they are lacking in intelligence. They are dependent on a shepherd or other animals such as dogs to herd them from place to place.

Sheep are often kept in an area known as a sheepfold at night. They are corralled into the fenced area through an entryway, which is guarded by the shepherd or a dog. This area may be rocky, full of sticks, weeds, and other types of plant growth. It becomes nasty and smelly from the dung of the sheep and the elements of the weather. Not a very pleasant place.

The sheep respond to the voice of their shepherd, knowing the voice that they are to trust. At nighttime, they follow his commands to settle into the sheepfold after coming in from the fields where they have been grazing. In the mornings, the sheep respond to the shepherd's voice as he calls them to leave the safety of their sheepfold and follow his lead to the fields.

Lessons from Jesus

Throughout the Bible, from the first book of Genesis through the last book of Revelation, there are many references to sheep and shepherds. The most important lesson is that we are to **follow Jesus, as sheep follow their shepherd.**

The scriptures in *John 10:1-5 NLT* illustrate all of the above so very clearly from both spiritual and agricultural perspectives, as Jesus said:

"I assure you, anyone who sneaks over the wall of a sheepfold, rather than going through the gate, must surely be a thief and a robber! For a shepherd enters through the gate. The gatekeeper opens the gate for him, and sheep hear his voice and come to him. He calls his own sheep by name and leads them out. And after he has gathered his own flock, he walks ahead of them, and they follow him because they recognize his voice. They won't follow a stranger; they will run from him because they don't recognize his voice."

Jesus then explains that he is the Good Shepherd for mankind in the verses *John 10:6-11 NLT.*

Those who heard Jesus use this illustration didn't understand what he meant, so he explained it to them. "I assure you. I am the gate for the sheep," he said. "All others who came before me were thieves and robbers. But the true sheep did not listen to them. Yes, I am the gate. Those who come in through me will be saved. Wherever they go, they will find green pastures. The thief's purpose is to steal and kill and destroy. My purpose is to give life in all its fullness."

"I am the good shepherd. The good shepherd lays down his life for the sheep."

In John 10:14 NIV, Jesus says,

"I am the good shepherd. I know my sheep and my sheep know me—just as the Father knows me and I know the Father—and I lay down my life for the sheep."

Update

Since I originally wrote this chapter, Alfreda has ceased working at the hospital lab in her original capacity. I miss seeing her welcoming presence when I go to that lab. She has returned to New Orleans because of her health and inability to continue working. She was very excited that her story was being included in this book. To God be the Glory!

CHAPTER 26

Giant Cell Arteritis and the Good Shepherd

As I wrote about my friend Alfreda and going to the hospital lab, I couldn't help but recall and reflect on the above scriptures about Jesus the Good Shepherd and us being his sheep. Jesus has been my shepherd as the **Giant Cell Arteritis (GCA) has ravaged my body, mind, and emotions. However, the disease has not ravaged my soul, because my Lord** has been with me every step of the way, leading me, as he leads the sheep.

I know His voice, as the sheep know his voice. I **listen for His voice**, and run from the foreign voices, as the sheep would do. I have stayed grounded in His Word through the Scriptures, music, prayer, and fellowship. When my eyesight prohibited reading the Word, I would depend on TV programs or scriptures hidden in my heart. On days when I couldn't pray—we all have those times—I would trust that I would hear God's voice in other ways. Since my immune system has been so compromised, I have been **confined to my home** most of the time since being diagnosed with GCA. So, most of my fellowship has been by way of the telephone or computer.

What Kind of Sheepfold? Tended or Dung-filled?

Being confined at home is somewhat analogous to the sheep staying in the sheepfold at night. It is the same place all the time and has the **tendency to become nasty if one does not take care** to keep it in order. As a patient, I needed care from others, as well as encouragement and compassion. My physical, mental, emotional, and spiritual needs all needed to be addressed. If they weren't, my life would become a dung-filled existence in all four realms.

What has helped us avoid existing in a dung-filled sheepfold and enabled us to keep on moving forward through this most difficult illness?

1. Jesus is the Good Shepherd in our family.
2. Listening for the voice of the Good Shepherd.
3. Being comforted in a compassionate way by others, who have learned the ways of the Good Shepherd.
4. Being thankful for people like Alfreda and her gift of compassion. Although it is unpleasant to constantly be going for medical care, we are so blessed to have caregivers who truly want to help and serve us.
5. Although we, as individuals, will never be the Good Shepherd, there are times that we will be called upon to be shepherds to other sheep. We will be leading others, in a compassionate or comforting way, with voices that those sheep will trust, knowing that the path they will follow will be the right one.

The following passage of Scripture illustrates the above points: Matthew 9:35–36 NLT "And wherever he went, he healed people of every sort of diseases and illness. He felt great pity for the crowds that came, because their problems were so great and they didn't know where to go for help. They were like sheep without a shepherd." I have depended on my shepherd throughout this journey with auto-immune diseases.

CHAPTER 27

Unexpected Blessings

This book would not be complete without giving credit to our Lord for His provision of completely unexpected blessings for they have been such an important part of my encouragement and healing through our journeys over the years. We give all the glory to Him and His servants and their obedience to His nudgings.

During my recovery process from the Giant Cell Arteritis illness, in the middle of the night, one night, while watching TV, the thought came to my mind that I should create a list of blessings that had been given to us during the recent months.

I grabbed an empty diary notebook and started making entries. Within a few minutes, I entered over twenty-five blessings. I was surprised how quickly I was able to create the list. Over the years, I have added to the list and as other events or items have happened, I have thought, "an addition to the **"unexpected blessings"** list. The blessings have been surprising in type and content. The variety has been endless. There are many verses scattered throughout the Bible that address the issue of God's provision of blessing us in our hours of need. Go into any Christian bookstore and you will find many books written about the subject matter.

Septic tank blessings

Our blessings have ranged from beautiful flower arrangements to funds to fix our "oh, so necessary" septic tank system. What a wide range of provisions! I do not want to bore you with a long-running list of gifts, but I would like to share with you the many ways God has provided His blessings to us in recent years.

In many ways, I have been given the opportunity to give back to others and utilize the gifts and talents that God had blessed me with. Often, all I had to do was think a little bit and realize how God was going to use me and still have my life be productive and give to others. **Rather than sitting in the corner, moaning and groaning about how useless I had become, it is your/ my responsibility to explore what you can do for others** in your weakened and disabled condition. In return, you become re-energized to expand your "new" life.

For example, in 1991, I was permanently injured by a drunk driver and my twenty-five year career as a CPA, Certified Public Accountant was abruptly ended. I say that God gave me a new career of working for Him in the field of Christianity, rather than continuing in the business field of accounting. It is amazing how my skills have been changed into new uses. **Do not be afraid of changes. Embrace it! You will be amazed at what gifts God has given you.**

Career changes

Previously, I had done a lot of teaching for my clients. In my disabled condition, I took up teaching adult Sunday school classes at our church, leading discussion groups, teaching classes for Stephen Ministry support programs, and other groups. I found that I enjoyed the change of venue. I also utilized my accounting skills for different programs within the church setting, including the Pre-school program and financial responsibilities for my local church at large. **The big change was my vocabulary.**

In my recovery stage, the **internet became my new home**. I became very active with support groups for others with the same or similar diseases or illnesses as mine. I became an **advocate for the importance of educating oneself and others** regarding these illnesses. I have had many nurses tell me that I have taught them much about practical everyday self-care with long-term, illnesses that do not have hope for being cured. With all this being said, **take time and effort to explore new ideas for yourself and others.** I now have friends in Australia, England, other parts of Europe, Africa, and all over the continental United States. I feel like a worldwide traveler with all these friends. I now identify with their locales when tragedies happen and feel **more in touch with the world at large.**

One day, while in the hospital, a nurse brought me a bouquet of flowers with the message that a hospital visitor gave them to her, saying that she should give them to someone to cheer them up. I was that grateful recipient.

It is commonly known that for most people it is **easier to give gifts and/or blessings than receive them**. Reluctance and/or embarrassment stand in the way of graciously or humbly receiving the blessing.

In the four Gospels of the New Testament, **Jesus is portrayed as the humble Servant and in the Old Testament; He is introduced in the role of Servanthood** to the reader. **God is referred to as Jehovah-jireh; the Lord who will provide.** Throughout the Scriptures, we are taught that the Lord will provide for our needs, which we refer to as blessings. In Matthew 6:7-8, Jesus instructed the people: "And when you are praying, do not use meaningless repetition, as the Gentiles do, for they suppose that they will be heard for their many words. Therefore, do not be like them: for your **Father knows what you need, before you ask Him**." Yet He instructs us to pray, "Give us this day our daily bread." Matthew 6:11.

In the Scriptures describing Holy Week, Jesus is portrayed in the role of Servanthood as He is involved in the process of **washing the feet of His disciples**. Foot washing was a common, humbling custom of the day, utilized to keep others feet clean from the elements of the streets. It was a blessing for the disciples, as Jesus cleaned their feet, as His one last act of kindness prior to their sharing Communion together before the end of His life and ministry on Earth. See Luke 7:44 and John 13:5-17 for Scriptural reference. Jim and I were humbled by friends, acting as Jesus, as we received many unexpected blessings in the early days of my illness. **It was up to us to accept these gifts/blessings from Jehovah-jireh, our provider and thank Him appropriately**. They are part of my list of twenty-five blessings referred to above.

Specific blessings

1. We traveled to Boston, in 2015, for a second opinion from a vasculitis specialist at Boston University. A few days prior to leaving home to drive to Boston, a friend from church appeared at our door. Jerry handed Jim an **envelope, with $200 in cash and said we might need it for taxi cab fees in Boston**. Recently, Jerry had suffered from heart infirmities and certainly didn't have money for such a gift for us. After he left, we kind of **snickered about needing taxi cab money**. When we arrived in Boston, they were experiencing a record two hundred year, front page newspaper worthy snowfall.

Roads were closed. Taxi cabs were shut down and if they did run, their insurance was not in effect. A scary thought.

Jim was determined he could drive the route from the hotel to the hospital. I convinced him that God had provided us with taxi cab money specifically, vis-a-vis Jerry, after I had been to the front desk of the hotel, and we were to use it for that. Besides that, **a cab driver was already available in the lobby**. All $200 was used for cab fees that week, as provided by Jehovah-jireh. **So much for our snickering**. Our hearts were changed and we had to confess our sinfulness.

When our taxi driver pulled out of our hotel parking lot and did some sliding, we **understood why Jim should not be driving** in Boston. Once on the streets, the driver realized certain main streets were closed. The driver knew of alternate routes, but Jim would not have.

Along our ride, he **told us about his day of 9-11**. That day he had taken a young lady to Boston airport to travel on a trip which she had won in a contest. Later that morning he learned she had been one of the victims flying on one of the planes that hit the World Trade Center in New York City. What a **sobering story to hear** as he told of the emotional strain it took on his life and his inability to work for the next two weeks. Immediately we were thrown into a mode of being compassionate to this kind taxi driver. Everyone in Boston must have a 9-11 story!

Our ride back to the hotel was an entirely different experience. We were tired and in a taxi with "Speedi Gonzalez", as we rode through the Boston Tunnel, under the Boston Bay. We slipped and slided through the ice and snow as Speedi was determined to earn as much as he could in this inclement weather. I saw **fear on Jim's face as he held on tightly to whatever he could grab.**

2. Our church has a **Prayers and Squares program of making quilts for shut-ins**. I was approached by one of the ladies, whom I had previously served as a Stephen Minister in her time of need, and asked if I would accept a quilt from the church and I was requested to create a prayer needs list. I gladly accepted the offered quilt and prayers. Sadly, this dear lady has since then passed on to Heaven from her own personal illnesses. I think of Sandy whenever I use the quilt. Today it resides on my hospital bed in our living room. The inscription date on my quilt is April 22, 2012.

3. Through some mutual contacts and Facebook, I had reconnected with one of my former dorm mates from my college days at CWRU in Cleveland, Ohio. We had often gone to her home during various college break times and were close friends. Her major had been in **speech therapy. She had established her own business and worked with patients with brain injuries.** I had explained to her **about my recent strokes and associated brain injuries that I had endured in 2012**. Tammy Beazell Story arranged to come visit with me in October, 2012 and helped to encourage me with my recovery from her home in Canada, which sits facing Lake Superior. What an unexpected blessing for me!

4. During this time, it was the time for my fiftieth anniversary of graduation from high school in 2012. I had been contacted by one of my childhood friends and classmates, Sara Jane Withers, notifying me of the event and a corresponding Facebook group. Through the Group, I became friends with several of the classmates. One of them, Judy Bogan, who lives in North Carolina, and I became close friends. I asked her to **review my writing for my books as I completed**

sections of them. One day she commented about us meeting each other and stated it would be in Heaven. When we were making plans to go to Boston, I called her and asked if we could stop and visit with her on our way back to Atlanta. She was totally surprised at my suggestion. When we met, it was as if we had been friends forever. Once again, God provided.

5.   **Patches**. Another day, the ladies with the "cheer cart" at the hospital gave me a small teddy bear that I named Patches, because of the patches sewn on it. That was a fun name for a bear that now sits on my computer table. Note that the title for book 2 is "Ugly Bears."

6.   **Sisters do help**. My younger sister Lois has been one of my unexpected blessings. Two years younger, she became **ill with lupus at age 25 in 1971.** I spent many days traveling to Detroit from Atlanta, with my two oldest children helping to take care of her when they were ages one to five. **Lois has been my cheerleader and caretaker, with visits and phone calls**. Lupus is similar to my giant cell Arteritis and accordingly, she has known how to support me in my needs. In the last few years, I have also been diagnosed with lupus. During several of my near-death experiences, she has been there to help my husband Jim and my adult children. When our mother died six years ago in 2014, she was there as the strong one, supporting me in the roles that I had to assume.

I have discussed all of this to say that support is not just meals, cards, visits, flowers, and phone calls for the sick. Granted each of the above is important in its own right, but there are other types of blessings that we can give to others. Just think about it.

Our **septic tank system malfunctioned** and as a result, part of our yard was dug up and a mess. For months, the area was unsightly as Jim worked at getting the system back in order. One day, he came in with a smile on his face and a check in his hand. Our **neighbor**

Jamie Shelton had given us funds to complete the project.
Another unexpected blessing. Certainly something that needed care,
when Jim was running back and forth to the hospital and doctor
appointments for me. Within a few days, our septic tank system was
rectified. This **same neighbor has prayed over me in the yard,**
while I have visited with him. What a blessing! What exciting events
and blessings have been ours, just because you have listened and been
aware as to what God has had in store for you in your journeys?
What surprises have you had? And can claim as blessings. More
importantly, what ideas are given to you to do for others to reflect
God's love? Just meditate and act.

Our daughter Janet's dream education was to attend Emory
University in Atlanta pursuing a degree in Religion. Her early
application was accepted and her only hurdle was to gather sufficient
funds to cover the pricey institution's tuition and other fees. Mom
and Dad submitted the customary parental financial aid forms and
as most parents find out, the colleges and government expect you to
graciously accept "college-poor" giving up all elements of fun in life.
Her grants and scholarships provided all but $1,500 of the needed
funds. What were we to do?

One hot summer day in Atlanta, a bad thunderstorm blew up,
twisting and turning the crop of pine trees in our backyard of two
acres. One **strike of lightning hit one of the larger pine trees**,
making a permanent vertical mark on its massive body. Our insurance
company deemed **the mark was worth $1,500** to the value of the
tree. For us, it meant that the $1,500 **needed for Janet's education
that semester was provided in a very profound and unique
way**. Who would have imagined that a lightning storm in 1988
would have done so at such a time in such a manner? Every time I
see that tree I am reminded of God's mighty and powerful ways of
providing when we least expect it. HOPE is always part of our lives.

Communicating with God in our own special ways is so very
important. **My Grandmother Haley would talk about wishing
that she had a direct telephone line to God in Heaven for
serious matters**. I think back to those days when people used to

listen to the conversations between people who shared common phone lines (party lines) and how their lines were interconnected. My Grandmother Haley would talk about **people sharing their deepest secrets over the phone lines and God being privileged to the most intimate secrets**. I even remember Grandma talking about such, when I was in my thirties. I can just imagine Grandma hearing about baby Mabry, the baby with potential birth defect problems. The following verse from the Message version of the Bible fits the situation: Jeremiah 33:3 "This is God's Message, the God who made earth, made it livable and lasting, known everywhere as GOD. "Call to me and I will answer you. I'll tell you marvelous and wondrous things that you could never figure out on your own."

The passage from the New Living Translation Matthew 6:25-34 is as follows:

Parable of the Birds

"So I tell you don't worry about everyday life—whether you have enough food, drink, and clothes. Doesn't life consist of more than food and clothing? Look at the birds. They don't need to plant or harvest or put food in barns because your heavenly Father feeds them. And you are far more valuable to Him than they are. Can all your worries add a single moment to your life? Of course not.

And why worry about your clothes? Look at the lilies and how they grow. They don't work or make their clothing.. yet Solomon in all his glory was not dressed as beautifully as they are. And if God cares so wonderfully for flowers that are here today and gone tomorrow, won't he more surely care for you? You have so little faith!

So don't worry about having enough food or drink or Why be like the pagans who are so deeply concerned about these things? Your Heavenly Father already knows all your needs, and He will give you all you need from day to day if you live for Him and make the Kingdom of God your primary concern.

So don't worry about tomorrow, for tomorrow will bring its own worries. Today's trouble is enough for today."

Tonight I was putting up the few items I had put out for the Christmas display. Among the items was the beautiful little bird you gave me several years ago, which I associate with this Scripture passage. When I saw the little bird, it reminded me once more of this story and its significance. Another way you fit into this story. Thank you. Thank you.

I am also suggesting that you read the discussion of untold blessings at the time of my mother's death as presented in the book "Ugly Bears" as a separate chapter. God was so good to us. Also read about giving some of my special rings (jewelry) to certain individuals in the story "Giving of the Rings" in the same book. It was an action near and dear to my heart, as a way of blessing others.

<u>Carrying out God's plan of sharing His comfort and compassion in the future.</u>

<u>See the discussion in "Ugly Bears."</u>

CHAPTER 28

Lemonade Activities

Lest you think our married life has been nothing but difficult times, I would like to let you know that Jim and I have enjoyed doing many activities together; exploring God's beautiful world amid the opportunities for exploration. Below is a brief outline of some of those journeys we have pursued together and/or with our children. I have named it Lemonade Activities because of our engagement story named "Lemons at the Beach."

- Walk to Emmaus and Kairos
- Photography
- Vacations
- Cooking and Baking

These activities have enhanced our marriage and grown our love for each other, as we have grown closer to each other in pursuing these times together. Some of them we have pursued in unconventional ways because of my illnesses, but that has made life more challenging and interesting. For example, when we visited Rocky Mountain National Park a few years ago, I placed my oxygen equipment in my wheelchair and pushed it along the trail around Bear Lake rather than carrying the oxygen equipment and having someone push me along the trail. Innovation and imagination were the name of the game. People along the trail told me I was an inspiration to them! No, they inspired me, telling me that!

CHAPTER 29

The Majesty of the Rising of the Butterfly's Journey

As you may have noticed each of the chapters of this book have included more than one person in the story. Years ago, I was part of a Walk to Emmaus support team and I was given the responsibility of giving the talk on the subject of Piety. Henri Nouwen, the author and theologian from Holland happens to be one of my favorite authors of his genre.

At the time I was preparing that talk, I received an advertisement that included a **quote from Henri Nouwen**. I decided to include the words in the talk and once again, I am going to include them in this chapter. The basic statement is that **our personal relationship with God shapes our married life**. (Refer back to the story "Lemons at the Beach.") **God woo's us to have a relationship**

with Him throughout our life. It is His desire that it be a **loving, intimate relationship with us, His unique creations, whom He created to interact with wholly and completely.**

Then God said, "Let us make people in our masters image, to be like ourselves. They will be masters over all life...........So God created people in His own image; God patterned them after himself; male and female he created them." Gen. 1:26-27 NLT (Note: It is assumed by many that "us" and "ourselves" is God and Jesus.)

In this Scripture in the beginning section of the Bible, the story of the creation of humans is presented. It also states that man is created in the image of God. Logically speaking, man has the characteristics of the personality and actions of God, as described in the Bible. Throughout the Scriptures, He urges mankind to follow in His ways and be like Him. You have probably noticed that throughout this book I have mentioned my Grandma Conklin and her spiritual influence upon my life. Basically, she taught me that my life is a journey and we are able to "rise above" our adversities or situations if we depend upon our Heavenly Father. She was my Mentor throughout my childhood and on into my adult life. She allowed God to "woo" her in her journey as she followed Him.

Personally, I like the word "woo", because it allows one's imagination to explore the concepts involved and relationships that may be developed. This book **"Rising Above"** has presented a group of events of adversities and the resulting comforting grace for the reader to contemplate and apply to their own lives and the related compassion to extend to others. It has been an experience of learning and motivation for the reader to become more spiritual and compassionate toward others in their everyday life. Let the Scripture verses presented above be your inspiration for your actions.

The purpose of this closing chapter is multi-fold:

- Present the *togetherness* **of the three children and their offspring**, from the marriage of Cloud M. Conklin, Sr. and his wife Mabel Morgan Conklin over the life span of their marriage of more than fifty years.

- Discuss the **diversity of the family, which eventually became a family of approximately one hundred individuals** *spread world-wide*, including Australia, Congo, Singapore, and many of the states in America. The family has truly been international in its activity since daughter Ruth began her mission work in the Congo in the 1940's. Some of the family have lived in other foreign lands over the years and will continue that course.

- Explore the concept of **God wooing Grandma Conklin and her devotion to mission work.**

- **Grandma's influence on her grandchildren and their children.** through such activities as cooking, sewing, and spiritual guidance, **reflecting a** *God-like life relationship*, including prayer, studying the Scriptures, meditation, and worship. Even in her waning years, she was a mentor to her grandchildren when she moved to California and was involved in their lives.

- The concept that *comforting others* **is an important part of our heritage.**

- *Mercy and social justice* are to be contemplated and carried forth from this family unit. These two issues are important to many of the grandchildren in their everyday work, activities and pursuits through many different avenues in our society.

- No matter where one lives, **education** is of paramount importance to that individual and others. At times, Grandma was a teacher in various school systems. Several of the grandchildren are or have been college professors, having earned PHD degrees in their chosen fields of study. Many of the grandchildren have become teachers in a wide variety of fields of study. Several of the grandchildren are published authors.

- Despite our differences, **unity** is important. The family is composed of a wide diversity of individuals in various areas of society, including religion (Christian, Jewish, Buddhist, atheist, and others), racial/ethic differences, political loyalty/interest, educational values and other standards. Through it all, we are a family unit that supports each other with love and compassion.

- **Life is a *journey***, as Grandma always said.
- As the **butterfly flies about, it *rises above* the conflicts and adversities, with Grace and love for us, teaching us to do so for others, in their time of need, in accordance with the principles of God's Word, the Holy Bible.**

My mother was due to celebrate her ninetieth birthday in June, 2011. My children decided we should have a **family birthday party** for their Mimi (Grandma). Eventually everyone decided it should become a **family reunion** and include their Boppa's (Grandpa Conklin-Mimi's husband) family. Boppa had died in 1974. Lois and I decided that we should host **the event at my house, with the Atlanta area being the venue** for the event. We started planning one year ahead of time because our **family lived all over the world. Logistics was the name of the game.**

The first decision was a date that would work for two of the cousins: **Carl Robinson from Sydney, Australia and Richard Bruce (Muk) Robinson from the Congo in Africa.** The other consideration was school calendars. Everyone else would have to make the date work. **Our most important goal was to have all the first cousins attend, since we had never had a family event with all of the first cousins in attendance before.** Next, I had to learn about Face book, so that I could communicate with the twelve cousins and start to make preliminary plans. I quickly learned that the family and extended family was much larger than I thought. Finding a hotel or resort for lodging for a three-day weekend was a chore unto itself.

As plans continued, it became evident that keeping a notebook with dividers was necessary. Also, I would have to divide responsibilities and corresponding titles. Additionally, Jim and I needed to remodel some of our forty year old house and refurbish our wooden back porch. Part of the back yard needed work done for the eating area.

After all my corresponding, it became evident that over sixty blood relatives were scheduled to attend the event scheduled as **the Conklin/Robinson Reunion celebrating Lorraine Conklin's ninetieth birthday** to be held at Jim and Bette's in Fayetteville, Georgia with our church Hopewell United Methodist Church being used on Saturday for one of the venues and the La Dolce Resort for lodging in Peachtree City, Georgia. Previously used as a corporate conference center, it was perfect with its lovely grounds and spacious areas for visitation areas in mid-June 2011.

Since most of us did not know each other very well, except for siblings, I had to come up with a way for the attendees to identify themselves. Additionally, I wanted to identify the blood relatives from the step-relatives and second marriages. By this time, there was a good bit of those types of relationships that existed. I decided to paint a family tree on one of the walls in our double car garage. It was the perfect place for the identifying marker. I did not include the family history extending back to the mid - 1640's when certain Conklin family members came to America by boat. Grandma (Mabel Morgan) and Gramps (Cloud McKinstry Conklin, Sr.) married and they had three children Caroline Ruth, George W, and Cloud McKinstry Conklin, Jr. listed in birth order. Ruth married Lawrence Robinson and they had five children: James, Carl Duncan, Elizabeth (Anne) Ruth, Richard Bruce, and Nina Lois. George W. married Olive van Wingerden and they had five children: Ruth, Willliam, Carole, Susan, and Anita. Cloud, Jr. married Elizabeth Lorraine Haley and they had two daughters Elizabeth (Bette) Lorraine and Lois Elaine. We had picnic tables set up in the garage and the back yard. The family tree was a focal point for discussion and understanding of how one was related to someone else. It was also a great background for taking photos.

Over the years, Lois and I were both well aware of the fact that there was a certain amount of disharmony that existed between Aunt Ruth, Uncle George, and Uncle Cloud. It was my desire that the weekend be held with as much unity and harmony as possible. Of course, Grandma wouldn't be there to see it, but it would please her. Accordingly, that thought guided all my planning. **U–N–I–T–Y!!!** The Reunion of Conklin and Robinson family members was scheduled to include over sixty people ranging in age from eight to ninety. Maintaining harmony was going to be a challenge. Fortunately, unity did appear to prevail throughout the weekend. **The Reunion strengthened our relationships for the future.** Carole, our wonder quilt maker, had breast cancer; Ira, the classy husband of Ruth, suffered a severe stroke and eventually passed; Bette suffered from auto–immune illnesses and had numerous surgeries and several near-death experiences. **The family members have rallied around each other, supporting each other with compassion**. In the past, there had been little interaction among the family members in such circumstances. Accordingly, Lois and I advocate that family Reunions are worth the work and effort to put together and attend.

Saturday Picnic at Hopewell Church, Photography Sessions

Saturday morning was time for the sixty-some relatives to spend getting acquainted with each other. The kids enjoyed the swimming pool and kept the schedule off-schedule. We had a Southern BarBQ facility prepare pork for us to serve as the entrée for our picnic that we held at our church grounds.

There was a covered pavilion with picnic benches which worked out well, especially when we had a major thunderstorm blow up on the extremely hot day. Hail and wind were part of the storm. Those from California were not used to hail and had a real experience seeing the hail storm, complete with loss of electricity. They scurried under the cover of the pavilion and into the closet areas to hide. It was comical to the rest of us. About that time our cousins from the Congo arrived after having been detained in their travels through

Belgium. They had been robbed and threatened by some thugs as they had been walking through the venues to get to their planes to fly to the United States. Needless to say, we had to stop everything and hear of their adventures from the bush country of Congo, through the unsafe areas of Europe.

We had also made arrangements for a professional photographer to come and capture the event on digital media for all of our safekeeping. He took over one hundred photo shots of the afternoon/evenings' event, providing us with lots of memories. Getting all of the family groups together was more like a three-ring circus or something like doing photos after a wedding. It provided much laughter.

One of the nicest things done was the making of a quilt by Cousin Carol Anderson for my mom. Everyone sent fabric to Carol. She pieced the quilt of many colors of blues, greens and purples. Her husband Chuck assembled and did the overstitching in a beautiful pattern for my mom. Cousin Anita made a crown for mom to wear, signifying her position as matriarch of the family, even though she was from the in-law side. That was very touching for my mom.

In our living room, we set up a display of Conklin family history. My father had created a family tree chart, extending from 1640 until the 1950's. The Conklin family had come to America from England in 1640 and ancestral records are available that have recorded those facts. The long scroll is interesting to look at, with all the sizeable families listed. Included is the name of Roscoe Conkling, who has a colorful political history, having potentially served in all three branches of the United States government before being killed for his unsavory social indiscretions. His appointment to the Supreme Court was controversial.

There was also one of the old family Bibles and several journals. Marriage certificates and other legal documents completed the assortment of interesting items along with photograph displays. An oval shaped photo of Clifford Cloud Conkling was hung on the wall. He was the inventor of the Coffer Dam method of building bridges (which is still used today) and his work is housed at the Smithsonian Museum in Washington DC.

Other old photos included one of Mary Jane Cloud, for whom my father and Gramps were named. The center piece photo was a family photo of Gramps Conklin, his three brothers (Clifford, Jack, and Bill) and their parents. The department store, high quality photo was produced in the early 1900's as a Christmas gift. The most exciting photo was of the Union soldier that Mary Jane Cloud was married to for a few short years before his death. A very lovely piece of art, it is in color, with a blue-colored frame.

To complete the collection of artifacts, we had my daddy's hard hat from working at NASA with the Space Program and his medals he won while competing in cross country track events, in the state of Ohio while in high school.

Sunday Impromptu Church Gathering and Time for "Rising Above"

Since Lois's husband was an active Methodist minister, we decided it would be nice to have a semi-church service for those who wanted to participate. The resort had an area that was similar to an arena/pavilion made with stone type steps and seating areas. It was a nice, outdoors worship area for us to use. Approximately fifty percent of those attending the weekend (30 people) came to worship jointly.

At the conclusion of his talk, Rev. Fred Finzer invited anyone who would like to say anything to do so. One of the first cousins volunteered and spoke with emotion about Grandma Conklin's influence on her life. She told that at a particular point in time, Grandma told her that she was on a journey and she (Sue) would "Rise Above" it. Grandma was an optimist and believer that life would work out. Since then, I have remembered the phrase "Rise Above" and understood its significance in my life and thus, the resulting title for this book. For those at the Reunion and who attended this family gathering, this was probably a highlight of the family time together. For those reading this book, may this chapter be a source of inspiration, be a provider of comfort/compassion to those in need, no matter how well you know the individual or how you care about them as a person. Always be on the watch for opportunities to make our world a better place by handing out love and grace through the gift of compassion. It's not difficult to do!

George Conklin's family- Chuck and Carol Anderson,
Ruth Rosenberg (d), Ira Rosenberg (d), Anita Amore,
Sue and David Howell, and Terry and Bill Conklin

Aunt Ruth and her five kids – Libby Robinson, Nina Robinson,
Jim Robinson, Aunt Ruth, Carl Robinson, Richard (Muk)
Robinson. These two groups of cousins were celebrating
Aunt Ruth's eighty something birthday in Denver, CO., in
June, 1996 with a glorious birthday party and and picnic.

CHAPTER 30

A Final Letter from Grandma Conklin

These are the final words from the last letter written by Grandma Conklin found in the files of my daddy. May they be as inspiring to each of you as they are to me. As I wrote in an earlier chapter, Grandma referred to death as the next journey in her life. The words in this letter reflect that theory of hers.

The instructions on the exterior of the envelope were to open the letter after she passed. Daddy noted on the envelope that it was received on December 5, 1968. She died November 23, 1971. It is with a humble heart and spirit that I pass this on to you. I am so thankful that I found this letter as I was in the process of writing "Rise Above." I praise God for Him allowing me to be His messenger. I find it especially interesting that Grandma refers to

Gramps prayer regarding us being made in God's image and the fact that in the chapter preceding this one (Chapter 29), I included the Scripture about God creating us in His image.

It is Thursday May 23 and this morning I had quite severe pain again that didn't seem to want to leave, but it finally did, and now I just have the weakness.

I have just read once more the scripture my loved one read on April 7, 1967 and I get new understanding each time I read it. The inevitability of death and God's power to lift us above our difficulties and those things we cannot help ourselves with. II Corinthians 4:8-18. And the prayer for that day could have been Cloud's especially. "O Thou Who hast made us in Thine image restore us that our witness may reflect Thy saving grace within us. Today we do not seek salvation, from suffering but from uselessness."

I know not when times will end for me but I feel as if I need to make each day count for some good. I am grateful for the life I have been privileged to have. I am sure the sorrows and hardships of the early years have helped to make me what I am. Christian friends have also helped to guide my life. I am grateful for a husband who was ever kind and thoughtful of my well-being.

I am grateful for my three children who have made me proud of them in many and different ways. Also of my numerous grandchildren who are finding their various stations in life and I pray will stay true to worthwhile ideals.

I am requesting no flowers except at the head and foot. The services may be as you wish but not elaborate.

This all seems so superfluous just now and I'll probably be here a long time. But I want you all to know my thoughts today. I only hope that most of all we have given you all strong Christian characters. I love you. Mother May 23, 1968

The Scripture Grandma is referring to in the above letter is as follows from the NIV Bible 2Cor 4:8-18:

We are hard pressed on every side, but not crushed; perplexed, but not in despair; persecuted, but not abandoned; struck down, but not destroyed. We always carry around in our body the death of Jesus, so that the life of Jesus may also be revealed in our body. For we who are alive, are always being given over to death for Jesus' sake, so his life may also be revealed in our mortal body. So then, death is at work in us, but life is at work in you.

It is written: "I believed; therefore I have spoken." With that same spirit of faith we also believe and therefore speak, because we know that the one who raised the Lord Jesus from the dead will also raise us with Jesus and present us with you in his presence. All this is for your benefit, so that the grace that is reaching more and more people may cause thanksgiving to overflow to the glory of God.

Therefore, we do not lose heart. Though outwardly we are wasting away, yet inwardly we are being renewed day by day. For our light and momentary troubles are achieving for us an eternal glory that far outweighs them all. So we fix our eyes not on what is seen, but on what is unseen. For what is seen is temporary, but what is unseen is eternal.

Spending my last days with Grandma Conklin in Denver hospital, prior to her gall bladder surgery, with slim chances of survival. She had never seen Janet and I was pregnant with Ricky.

Wedding of Eve Thompson and Richard Robinson in north Miami on 12/29/07. Guests included nieces, nephews, aunts, uncles, siblings, and children of groom.

Cousin Carl Robinson and his lovely Vietnamese wife Kim
Dung, from Sydney, Australia at the birthday celebration
for Aunt Ruth, his mother. Our first trip to Colorado
and opportunity to meet many of the family.

Our son Richard Mabry and his beautiful daughter Jewel
Mabry as part of Junior Year Homecoming Court, Lamar
County High School, Barnesville, GA, 10/18.

Grandma and Gramps Conklin at New York City Harbor
with grandchildren Jim, Carl, and Libby Robinson on
their way to Congo in 1948. A long trip from Ohio,
Grandma is dressed up in dress and hat, as is Gramps in
suit and tie to send daughter Ruth to mission work.

CHAPTER 31

Appendix

Key Scriptures for the Book

Following are Scriptures for study in association with the stories in this book and further clarification of other Scriptures within both of the books I have written.

> [9]For this reason, since the day we heard about you, we have not stopped praying for you and asking God to fill you with the knowledge of His will through all spiritual wisdom and understanding. [10]And we pray this in order that you may live a life worthy of the Lord and may please Him in every way: bearing fruit in every good work, growing in the knowledge of God, [11]being strengthened with all power according

to his glorious might so that you may have great endurance and patience, and joyfully [12]giving thanks to the Father, who has qualified you to share in the inheritance of the saints in the kingdom of light. [13]For he has rescued us from the dominion of darkness and brought us into the kingdom of the Son He loves, [14]in whom we have redemption, the forgiveness of sins.

Colossians 1:9-14 NIV

[3]Praise be to the God and Father of our Lord Jesus Christ, the Father of compassion and the God of all comfort, [4]who comforts us in all our troubles, so that we can comfort those in any trouble with the comfort we ourselves have received from God. [5]For just as the sufferings of Christ flow over into our lives, so also through Christ, our comfort overflows. [6]If we are distressed, it is for your comfort and salvation, if we are comforted, it is for your comfort, which produces in you patient endurance of the same sufferings we suffer. [7]And our hope of you is firm, because we know that so also you share in our sufferings so also you share in our comfort.

2 Corinthians 1:3-7 NIV

Now to Him who is able to do immeasurably more than all we ask or imagine, according to His power that is at work within us, to Him be glory in the church and in Christ Jesus throughout all generations forever and ever. Amen.

Ephesians 3:20-21 NIV

Do not conform any longer to the pattern of this world, but be **transformed by the renewing of your mind**. Then you will be able to test and approve what God's will is — His good, pleasing, and perfect will.

Romans 12:3 NIV

Trust in the Lord with all your heart,
And lean not on your own understanding.
In all your ways acknowledge Him
And He shall direct your paths.

Prov. 3:5-6 NKJV

A **merry heart** does good, **like medicine**.

Prov. 17:22 NKJV

I have come that they may **have life**, and that they may have it **more abundantly**.

John 10:10 NKJV

Therefore, whatever you want men to do to you, do also to them. Then Jesus spoke to them again, saying, "**I am the light** of the world. He who **follows Me shall not walk in darkness**, but have the light of life."

John 8:12 NKJV

Perseverance must finish its work so that you may be mature and complete, not lacking anything. If any of you lacks **wisdom**, he should ask God who **gives generously** to all without finding fault, and it will be given to him. But when he asks, he must **believe** and not doubt, because he who doubts is like a wave of the sea, blown and tossed by the wind. That man should not think that he will receive anything from the Lord; he is a double-minded man, unstable in all he does."

James 1:2-8 NIV

My brethren, count it all **joy** when you fall into various trials, knowing that the testing of your **faith produces patience**. But let patience have its **perfect work**, that you may be perfect and complete, **lacking nothing**. If any of you lacks **wisdom**, let him ask of God, who gives to all liberally and without reproach, and it will be given to him. But let him **ask in faith**, with no doubting, for he who doubts is like a wave of the sea driven and tossed by the wind. For let not that man suppose that he will receive anything from the Lord, he is a double-minded man, unstable in all his ways.

James 1:2-8 NKJV

Printed in the United States
By Bookmasters